1000 FANTASTIC FACTS

Written by Anne McKie and Angela Royston.
Edited by Melanie J. Clayden.
Ilustrated by Ken McKie.

© 1995 Grandreams Limited

Published by
Grandreams Limited
Jadwin House, 205/211 Kentish Town Road,
London, NW5 2JU.

Printed in Czech Republic.

This book belongs to:

....

....

....

....

Age:.........................

A MIGHTY MILLION 1,000,000

A million is a mighty big number, but do you know how big? This block has 100 stars in it.

1,000 stars would take up the whole page. To show 1,000,000 stars you would need to cover the floor, the walls and the ceiling of an average sitting room (4m by 3m by 2.5m high/13ft by 10ft by 8ft high).

How thick would a book with a million pages be?
This book has 96 pages. If a book had a million pages it would be 70m thick - as high as a 23-storey skyscraper!

A millionaire is someone who owns £1 million. If a millionaire changed all their money into £1 coins and piled them up on top of one another, how high do you think they'd reach? The answer is at the bottom of the page.

A colossal Mini traffic jam.
The Mini is one of Britain's best selling cars. Over five million have been sold since the first one was produced back in 1959. Suppose one million Minis set off from Edinburgh south to London and on across the channel towards Germany. Each Mini is 3m (10ft) long. Suppose they travelled bumper to bumper with no space between them, how far do you think the first car would have gone before the last car started? The answer is at the bottom of the page.

Answer: The millionaire's pile would be 3,000m (9,843ft) high. That's more than twice as high as Britain's tallest mountain (Ben Nevis) and nearly a third as high as Mount Everest, the highest mountain in the world.

Answer: Mini jam: the first car would have reached Moscow 3,000km (1,875 miles) away.

A million people - how many is that?

In 1916 in the First World War one million men were killed in one battle, the battle of the Somme. In Britain in 1992 over three million people were unemployed. Suppose a million people decided to march in rows of four, 1.5m (5ft) apart, from Trafalgar Square in London, north to the M1, where do you think the front of the column would be when the last people left? Would they reach the M1 at all? Would they reach St. Albans, 32km (23 miles) from London? Or would they get farther?

Answer: A million people: the front of the column would have marched 375km (234 miles) before the millionth person left Trafalgar Square. They would have passed through Leeds and be within 6km (4 miles) of Richmond in North Yorkshire.

A trip in a million.

What were you doing one million seconds ago? That was 11 days, 20 hours, 4 minutes and 4 seconds ago?

What were you doing a million minutes ago? That's nearly two years ago - one year, 345 days, 4 hours, 4 minutes precisely.

You weren't doing anything a million hours ago, but if you could go back in time you would find yourself in the Victorian age, 114 years, 28 days and 16 hours ago. There were steam trains and the car was just about to be invented, but there was no television, no computers and you didn't have to go to school.

If you travelled back to a million days ago, you would find yourself in about 744 BC. Christ had not been born and the Roman Empire had scarcely begun.

A million weeks ago would take you back to 17,000 BC. Britain and northern Europe were covered with ice. Elsewhere people lived in caves and hunted for food.

A million years ago, there were people only in Africa. Prehistoric animals such as the sabre-toothed tiger roamed the land, but no dinosaurs. They had already died out 64 million years before!

An old advertisement began, "A million housewives every day pick up a can of beans..." If they put all their baked beans together, could they fill a bath tub? $10\frac{1}{2}$ bath tubs? A public swimming pool? Answer below.

Answer: Baked bean bonanza: a million cans of baked beans would fill a swimming pool 25m by 13.5m to a depth of 1.5m (82ft by 44ft by 5ft).

If you piled a million soft drink cans one on top of the other, how high would they reach?

1) as high as Mount Everest (8,848m/29,030ft)?
2) 110km (68 miles) into the ionosphere where satellites orbit?
3) 384,402km (238,867 miles), right to the Moon itself?

Answer: The soft drink cans would reach 110km (68 miles). Not to the Moon - even the fizziest drink is not that spectacular!

CONTINENTS, MOUNTAINS AND ROCKS

Continents fit together like pieces of a vast jigsaw. At one time (220 million years ago) all the continents were part of one supercontinent, which we now call Pangaea. The land is made up of huge blocks which float on a sea of lava (molten rock). Slowly Pangaea broke up and the continents drifted away from each other. They are still moving.

The biggest continent in the world is Asia. It is nearly five times larger than Australia, the smallest continent. Africa and Asia together account for just over half of all the land in the world.

Asia: 43.6 million sq. km (16.8 million sq. miles); Africa: 30.3 million sq. km (11.6 million sq. miles); North America: 25.3 million sq. km (9.7 million sq. miles); South America: 17.8 million sq. km (6.8 million sq. miles); Antarctica: 14 million sq. km (5.4 million sq. miles); Europe: 10.5 million sq. km (4 million sq. miles); Australasia: 8.9 million sq. km (3.4 million sq. miles).

The Atlantic Ocean is getting wider. North America is drifting away from Europe but only very slowly at 1cm (0.39in) a year.

The top 109 highest mountains in the world are all in Asia and 96 of them are in the Himalayas.

Mount Everest is the highest mountain of land. It is 8,848m (29,030ft) high. That is 20 times as high as the Sears Tower in Chicago. If an office block was as high as Mount Everest it would have 2,200 storeys! (If you jumped off Mount Everest it would take you two minutes and 43 seconds to hit the ground.)

The first people to climb to the top of Mount Everest were Edmund Hillary, a New Zealand mountaineer, and Sherpa Tenzing on 29th May, 1953.

Snow at the Equator.

Mount Kenya is on the Equator, but its peak, 5,199m (17,058ft) above sea level, is always covered in snow.

As you climb a mountain, the temperature drops and the climate changes as if you were going to the North or South Pole. If you climbed Mount Kenya you would leave the elephants and grassland at sea level, climb through tropical rainforest at around 1,650m (5,413ft), then through bamboo and heathland (watch out for the leopards up here), before reaching alpine grassland towards the summit.

Mount Snowdon in Wales, was once as high as the mountains of the Alps (over 5,000m/16,405ft) but ice, wind, rain and snow have gradually worn it down to its present height of 1,085m (3,560ft).

The island of Hawaii is the peak of a large mountain which is even bigger than Mount Everest. The base of Hawaii's mountain is 9,000m (29,529ft) below sea level on the ocean floor.

A monster in the mountains.

Huge footprints have been found in the snow of the Himalayas and some people claim to have seen a monster, half person, half monkey, but no-one has ever captured such a creature. The most likely explanation is that the prints were made by the huge Moon bear.

The lowest dry land in the world is the shore of the Dead Sea between Israel and Jordan. It is 400m (1,312ft) below sea level. If there was a flight of stairs to take you back up to sea level you would have to climb 2,000 steps. Try climbing your own stairs that number of times and you will soon see how tiring it gets!

The largest cave in the world is the Sarawak Chamber in Sarawak, Malaysia. Its floor area is 210,000 sq. m (2,260,440 sq. ft), about the same size as three soccer pitches put together. Its roof is at least 70m (230ft) high, about as high as a 23 storey building.

The longest system of caves is in Kentucky in the United States. You can walk under the ground here along passages and through caves for over 530km (329 miles), that is the same distance as walking from Southampton to Carlisle - the whole length of England.

Ayer's Rock in central Australia is one big chunk of rock 335m (1,099ft) high. It is much larger than all the other boulders in the surrounding desert, but not as large as Mount Augustus in Western Australia, another big rock, 1,105m (3,625ft) high.

The oldest rocks in the world are in Western Australia. They date from 4,300 million years ago, only 300 million years after the Earth was formed.

ISLANDS, LAKES, RIVERS AND WATERFALLS

The most isolated islanders.

The people who live on Tristan da Cunha are over 2,000km (about 1,300 miles) from their nearest neighbours on the island of St Helena. That's nearly as far as Moscow is from London. Tristan da Cunha is in the South Atlantic Ocean nearly 3,000km (1,864 miles) from the southern tip of Africa. Tristan da Cunha has an active volcano and in 1961 all the islanders had to leave before they were swamped with lava. It was two years before 198 of them returned to the island.

An island from nowhere.

In 1963 the sea to the south west of Iceland began to boil and bubble. Slowly the island of Surtsey rose through the water. It was made of molten lava from a volcano. The lava cooled and plant seeds blown across the sea soon began to grow there.

Islands made of shells.

Coral reefs are made up of the skeletons of millions of tiny animals. Sometimes the reef forms a circle, or atoll, with sea water in the middle.

The world's largest island.

Greenland is the world's largest island. (Australia is a continent and so it doesn't count). Greenland is just over 2,000,000 sq. km (1,242,800 sq. miles), nearly ten times as large as Great Britain. It is covered with ice and snow.

New Guinea, Borneo and Madagascar are the three next biggest islands, but they could all fit into Greenland.

The largest freshwater lake in the world is Lake Superior in Canada. It is just over 80,000 sq. km (30,888 sq. miles), bigger than the whole of Holland and Belgium put together. The Caspian Sea is even larger - nearly five times larger than Lake Superior - but its waters are salty.

Lake Malawi takes up one quarter of the whole country of Malawi.

Lake Baikal in central Siberia is the deepest lake in the world. It is 1940 metres deep, more than twice as deep as the North Sea. Canary Wharf is Europe's tallest office building, but Lake Baikal is eight times as deep as it is tall. Lake Baikal has more water in it than any other lake - 23,000 cubic km of it. It could drown the whole of Great Britain up to a depth of about 100m (328ft). Only buildings more than 30 storeys high would show above the surface of the water.

Lake with a monster.

Is there a monster in Loch Ness? Several people say they have seen it, but whenever scientists investigate, Nessie hides. There is no scientific evidence that Nessie exists, but hundreds of tourists go every year to see for themselves.

Longest river.

The world's longest river is the Nile. It flows from central Africa 6,670km (4,145 miles) north to the Mediterranean Sea. If all the bends were straightened out it would reach about one third of the distance from the North Pole to the South Pole.

The longest river in the United Kingdom is the River Severn. At only 354km (220 miles) long it is a mere stream compared with the world's greatest rivers.

The muddiest river in the world is the Hwang Ho in China. It carries so much silt you could build a vast wall 40m (131ft) high and 6m (20ft) wide all round the world.

The African name for the Victoria Falls on the border between Zaire and Zimbabwe is 'The Smoke That Thunders'. You can see the huge cloud of spray that rises high into the air from 32km (20 miles) away, long before you can hear the thundering of the water.

Angel Falls in Venezuela is the highest waterfall in the world. It drops 979m (3,212ft), two and a half times the height of the Empire State Building (381m/1,250ft) and more than four times the height of Canary Wharf (228m/748ft).

DESERTS

The Sahara Desert is the largest desert in the world. It is bigger than the four next largest deserts put together. It is as vast as the whole of the United States of America including most of Alaska and nearly as big as the whole of Europe.

Sahara: 9 million sq. km (3.5 million sq. miles); Australian: 3.4 million sq. km (1.3 million sq. miles); Arabian: 2.6 million sq. km (1 million sq. miles); Turkestan: 1.9 million sq. km (0.7 million sq. miles); Great American Desert: 1.3 million sq. km (0.5 million sq. miles)

The Sahara Desert was once green with trees and plants. Giraffes, elephants and rhinos wandered across it. We know this because they are shown in rock paintings found in south-east Algeria, drawn thousands of years ago.

Even as recently as the 1820s a French explorer heard lions roaring in thick forest where now there is only desert.

The world's deserts are growing bigger. The Sahara is growing by 1.5 million hectares (4.1 million acres) every year. That is an area three quarters the size of Wales every year, or four football pitches every minute.

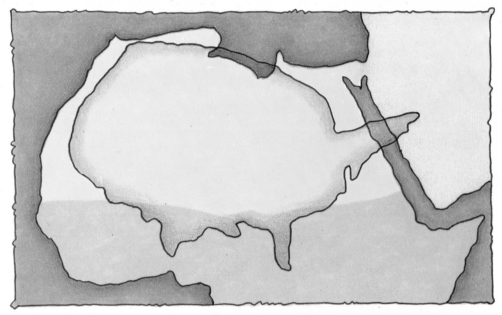

The shaded area shows how the U.S.A. could fit into the Sahara Desert.

The driest desert is the Atacama Desert in northern Chile, South America. Until 1971 it had had no rain at all for 400 years.

The foggiest desert is the Namib Desert in Namibia, south-west Africa. Most of the moisture it receives drifts in as fog from the Atlantic Ocean.

During the day the sand gets very hot, up to 90°C (195°F). That is almost hot enough to boil water and too hot for alcohol. It

changes into a vapour around 80°C (176°F).

An oasis is a spring of water in the desert. Sometimes desert travellers think they see a pool of water where there is none. This is called a mirage, but they have not just imagined it. It is caused by a trick of the light in which part of the blue sky appears to be surrounded by land.

The biggest sand dunes are in Algeria in the Sahara Desert. They are up to 430m (1,411ft) high, nearly three times the height of the Great Pyramid of Cheops in Egypt or nearly twice as high as Canary Wharf.

One of the greatest hazards of travelling through the desert (apart from dying of heat and thirst) is getting caught in a sand storm. Every year up to 200 million tonnes of sand is blown from the Sahara into the Atlantic Ocean. That is enough to make an enormous sand castle over central London as high as the Alps (5,000m/16,405ft).

Deserts have many poisonous snakes or scorpions, but few people are killed by them. More people die from mosquito bites than from all the other bites and stings put together.

The tallest cacti are the giant saguaros. They grow up to 18m (59ft) tall, about the height of a six-storey building.

Baobab trees become fatter or thinner depending on the weather. When it rains the roots drink in the water and the tree stores it in the trunk. During the long dry season the tree becomes thinner and thinner as it uses up its store of water.

Hairy running shoes!
Gerbils have hairy feet to protect them from the hot sand. They bound along with their feet hardly touching the sand.

Camels can go for several days without food or water. They carry a supply of fat in their humps. A camel with a sagging hump is a hungry camel! They lose no water from their bodies. They do not sweat and their urine is solid crystals.

Desert plants often have very long roots. They need them to catch all the moisture they can. Some desert acacias have roots which probe 15m (49ft) below the ground. If the tree were growing on the roof of a five-storey house the roots would touch the ground.

People in the desert do not wash-up with water - they use sand to clean their dirty dishes.

OCEANS, WAVES AND SEA

Nearly three quarters of the Earth is covered by sea.

The Pacific Ocean is the largest ocean and covers nearly half of the world (about 46%). If aliens from outer space saw Earth from this angle they would think the Earth was covered with water.

The Arctic Ocean is entirely covered with ice for the whole of the winter.

Underwater world.
What is at the bottom of the sea? Mountains and valleys and flat plains, like on land. A range of mountains runs right down the middle of the Atlantic from the Arctic almost to Antarctica.

The continental shelf.
The sea around most continents is only about 180m (590ft) deep - that is deep enough to cover all the skyscrapers in the City of London except the Natwest Tower and Canary Wharf.

The ocean floor.
Don't fall off the continental shelf! It ends abruptly some distance from the coast. The ground then drops down the continental slope to the ocean floor about 3,600m (11,812ft) below. You could sink two Ben Nevis's on the ocean floor and still have 1,000m (3,281ft) of clear water above them.

Ocean trenches.
In places the floor plunges even deeper, into cracks and trenches. The deepest trench is the Marianas Trench in the Pacific Ocean. The bottom is 11,000m (36,091ft) below the surface, deep enough to sink Mount Everest, the world's highest mountain and still have nearly 2,200m (7,218ft) of water to spare.

The ocean floor is completely dark. Very few fish can live there. The black angler fish is one that does. It carries its own lantern to lure prey into its huge mouth. The light is made by bacteria that glow in the dark.

The Mediterranean Sea is closing up, but very slowly. Every year North Africa moves a centimetre or two closer to Italy, Greece and France.

The saltiest seas are in the Middle East where the hot sun beats down evaporating the water and making it saltier and saltier. The Red Sea is so salty you cannot sink - the salt keeps you floating!

The biggest waves are produced when a storm pushes a big mid-ocean wave into shallower coastal waters. The biggest wave ever recorded was 34m (111ft) high - as high as a 10-storey building.

In July 1978 Walter Poenisch swam from Cuba - an island in the Caribbean Sea - to Florida in the United States. The waters are so dangerous he swam inside a shark cage and took just over 34 hours to complete the 207km (129 mile) journey.

The first person to swim the 34km (21 miles) across the English channel from Dover to Calais was Matthew Webb. He swam for 21 hours 45 minutes and reached France at 10.41 on the 25th August, 1875.

The Irish Channel between Scotland and Northern Ireland is much the same distance, 37km (23 miles), but has stronger currents, very cold water, and is much harder to swim. The first person to do so was Tom Blower who took 15 hours 26 minutes in 1947.

The highest cliffs in the world are in Hawaii. They rise just over 1,000m (3,281ft) from the sea - that is nearly four times as high as Canary Wharf. If you threw a huge stone off the top, it would take about 15 seconds before you heard the splash.

There are two high tides every day. The highest high tides are in the Bay of Fundy between Nova Scotia and New Brunswick on the east coast of Canada. Here the water level at high tide can be 14.5m (47ft) above that at low tide - that is nearly as high as a five-storey house.

The highest tides in Britain are on the Severn Estuary, just where the M4 crosses the river. Here, the high tide mark can be nearly 12.5m (41ft) above the low tide - nearly deep enough to cover three double decker buses, one on top of the other.

Waves are caused by the wind blowing on the sea. Waves can travel thousands of kilometres, provided there is no land in the way to stop them. Waves which begin in the Indian Ocean may travel 19,000km (11,807 miles) all the way to Alaska.

ICE AND SNOW

The biggest iceberg ever spotted was floating off Antarctica in 1956. It was 31,000 sq. km (11,969 sq. miles) in area. This is as large as the whole country of Belgium.

Wealthy Arab countries have considered towing icebergs from the Antarctic to their desert states in the Middle East. Much of the ice would melt, of course, as the iceberg was towed across the Equator, but enough would remain to provide a much needed supply of water.

Icebergs are made by glaciers. Glaciers are rivers of ice which slowly flow into the sea. As another huge chunk of ice breaks off the end into the sea, a new iceberg floats away. Greenland's glaciers alone produce 14,000 icebergs each year.

The longest glacier in the world is the Lambert glacier in Antarctica. It is over 400km (249 miles) long. If it were moved to Britain you could skate all the way from Glasgow to Birmingham.

The fastest glacier is in Greenland. It moves about 1m (3.3ft) every hour.

An iceberg that sunk the unsinkable.
In 1912 the Titanic hit an iceberg and sunk, drowning about 1,500 people. Although everyone thought the ship was unsinkable, it sank on its first voyage.

Ice covers one tenth of the surface of the oceans.

Britain was once covered with ice, just like Greenland is today. During the last Ice Age, 10,000 years ago, the polar icecap covered much of northern Europe, Canada and northern Asia.

Antarctica is covered with ice which, on average, is 2,000m (6,562ft) thick. You could sink Ben Nevis (Britain's highest mountain) in it and still have 657m (2,156ft) of ice to spare.

No-one lives on Antarctica - except penguins, seals and a few scientists and engineers.

Antarctica is a desert. It gets very little rain or snow, but plenty of wind. It is the coldest place on Earth. In July 1983 the temperature dropped to -83°C (-117°F) at Vostock station.

The first men to reach the Poles.
Robert Peary claimed in 1909 that he was the first person to reach the North Pole.

Two explorers raced to reach the South Pole first. Roald Amundsen from Norway reached the Pole in December 1911 and won the race. Captain Scott from Britain reached it a month later in January 1912. Unfortunately, he and his party froze to death before they reached their base camp again.

Midnight Sun.
Inside the Arctic circle and on Antarctica it never gets properly dark for 147 days in summer. For several months in the winter it never gets properly light!

If all the ice on Antarctica melted, sea level would rise all over the world by 60m (197ft). Coastal towns and cities would all be drowned and vast areas of land lost, including most of Holland, Belgium and Bangladesh.

Even if the sea level only rose by 5m (16ft), most of Florida and many other American cities would be drowned.

Every snowflake has a different pattern.

RAIN, WIND AND STORMS

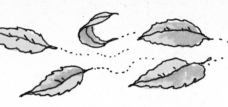

Too hot for comfort.
Be thankful you were not in Death Valley in the Californian Desert during July 1971. For six weeks the temperature there reached 49°C (120°F) every day - and that was in the shade!

If you lived in Wyndham in western Australia you would get used to hot weather. The temperature is over 32°C (90°F) on almost every day of the year - nearly as hot as the hottest temperature ever recorded in Britain (36.8°C or 98°F).

Rain, rain and more rain.
On Mount Waialeale in Hawaii it rains nearly every day. In fact there are only about 15 days every year when it doesn't rain. Ballynahinch in Galway is not much drier. It has up to 309 rainy days a year.

Worst rain shower in the world.
Just under 2m (6ft) of rain fell in one day on La Reunion in the Indian Ocean in March 1962.

The wettest place of all is Tutunendo in Colombia, South America. Nearly 12m (39ft) of rain falls there every year. That's more than six times as deep as the average swimming pool.

Great deluge.
The longest shower of rain ever lasted 60,000 years. It occurred about 4,000 million years ago and created all the seas and oceans.

The Pole of Cold.
Antarctica has all the lowest temperatures in the world. The coldest place is called the Pole of Cold. Here the average temperature during the year is nearly -58°C (-72 °F). On many days it is much colder!

Nobody lives at the Pole of Cold, but a few thousand people live in the small town of Oymyakon in Siberia. Here the temperature has been known to drop to -68°C (-98°F). Not the best place for a winter holiday!

Fast as lightning.

The fastest flashes move at 140,000km per second (87,000 miles per second) - fast enough to go three times round the Equator in one second, but of course lightning does not travel that far. The longest flashes of lightning are about 30km (19 miles) from cloud to ground.

If you want to know how far away a thunderstorm is, see how many times you can count slowly up to five between the flash and the rumble. Every group of five equals a mile. Count in groups of three to get kilometres.

If you don't like thunderstorms don't go near the Tropics. There are over 3,000 thunderstorms somewhere in the Tropics, or nearby, every night. Bogor in Java has thunder on up to 320 nights every year.

How big are the heaviest hailstones?

As big as a golf ball? No, much bigger. In April 1986, huge balls of ice fell from the sky and crashed to the ground in Gopalganj in Bangladesh. They weighed nearly 1kg (2.2lbs) and must have been about the size of small honeydew melons. They killed 92 people.

The heaviest snowstorm fell on Mount Shasta in California. For six days it never stopped snowing and at the end, the snow was nearly 5m (16ft) deep.

Winters used to be colder.

In Britain the Thames used to freeze and people held fairs on the ice. The last one was held in 1814.

Warming up or cooling down?

Some scientists warn that another Ice Age is on the way. In a thousand years time Britain and much of northern Europe, America and Asia may be covered with snow and ice all year round.

In the meantime the Earth is getting warmer. Cars, trucks, factories and power stations are polluting the air with carbon dioxide. This gas hangs in the air and forms a warm blanket around the Earth keeping in the heat. But don't think the weather will get better as the Earth warms up. There will be more storms, hurricanes and droughts. Much of southern Europe will become like the Sahara.

Tornadoes seldom last more than an hour and move very slowly across the country. Yet in that time they do tremendous damage. In 1925 a tornado killed 700 people in south-central United States of America.

The world's worst hurricane hit Bangladesh in November 1970. A million people were killed by the floods whipped up by the winds and the rain.

It has never actually rained cats and dogs, but it has rained fish! Sometimes fish are sucked up by a tornado, like a vacuum cleaner sucking up dust. The fish can be carried a long way in the wind before dropping to the ground.

The highest winds are whipped up by tornadoes. In 1958 winds of 450 kilometres per hour (280 miles per hour) hit Wichita Falls in Texas, USA. That is faster than the fastest passenger train and as fast as a racing car.

VOLCANOES, GEYSERS AND EARTHQUAKES

In 1883 a volcanic island in Indonesia, called Krakatoa, erupted. Over 150 villages were destroyed and the sound of the eruption could be heard in Australia, 5,000km (3,107 miles) away.

Greatest eruption ever known.

In 1470 BC the Greek Island of Santorini erupted with five times the force of Krakatoa. The power of the eruption is estimated to be 130 times greater than the biggest bomb ever detonated. The whole island was destroyed and a massive tidal wave overwhelmed Crete. This huge wave may have wiped out all the Minoan people who lived there.

In 1815 Tambora, another volcano in Indonesia, erupted. One hundred and fifty three cubic km of rock was blown out, leaving the island 1,250m (4,101ft) lower than before. That is enough rock to cover the whole of England and Wales to a depth of 1m (3ft), or the whole of Scotland with 2m (6ft) of rocks and debris.

The island of Vulcano, just off Sicily, is no longer an active volcano. You can sunbathe on its beaches in perfect safety, but you may feel that you are sunbathing on an open cast coal mine. The sand is ancient lava and is quite black, like coal dust.

What causes volcanoes and earthquakes?

The Earth's crust floats on a sea of hot, molten lava. The crust is weaker in some places and here the hot magma may force its way through the crust to the surface.

There are 850 volcanoes in the world, many of them beneath the sea. There are also about 1,000 earthquakes every year that are strong enough to be felt. The Earth's crust is divided into plates which move on the molten lava. Most earthquakes and volcanoes occur where one plate is pushing against another. There is plate movement all around the edge of the Pacific Ocean, creating a 'ring of fire'.

There are no active volcanoes in the United Kingdom, but several extinct ones. There are Earth tremors every few days but only a few of them are strong enough to be felt. The largest one measured 5.1 on the Richter Scale. It was centred on Bishop's Castle on the Welsh/Shropshire border and the shock wave was felt all over Wales and England and even in Dublin in Eire. An earlier Welsh earthquake in 1984 measured 5.4 on the Richter Scale and was felt as far away as southern Scotland.

The largest volcano still active today is Mauna Loa in Hawaii. Its crater is about 3.5km (2.1 miles) across and is more than 150m (492ft) deep. It erupts about once every 3¹/₂ years. If Trafalgar Square were on one edge, the Monument in the City of London would be on the other side.

Tidal waves have nothing to do with the tide. They are caused by earthquakes or volcanoes. They can travel for thousands of kilometres. In 1960 an earthquake in Chile whipped up a giant wave which travelled right across the Pacific Ocean and swamped towns and villages in Japan. This Chilean earthquake is probably the largest ever recorded.

The highest known wave was 67m (219ft) high. This is nearly half as high again as Nelson's Column in Trafalgar Square, London. It was generated by a mighty earthquake in Alaska in 1964 that measured 8.9 on the Richter Scale.

Thousands of people have been killed by earthquakes. When the most destructive earthquake shook Shensi Province in China in 1556, about 800,000 people died. Nearly as many may have died in 1976 in Tangshan, again in China. The exact number of deaths in this earthquake is not known because the Chinese government have concealed the extent of the damage.

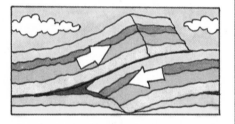

The Earth's surface is made up of 'plates'. These are moving slightly all the time. When pressure builds up between two plates the result is an earthquake.

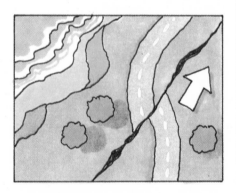

Animals often know that an earthquake is going to happen before people do. There are many stories of animals alerting their owners and saving them from harm. The animals can probably detect the slight tremors that precede the main earthquake.

Geysers are hot springs which shoot spouts of steam and hot water up to 30m (98ft) into the air. They occur where underground water is heated by pockets of magma. Freezing Icelanders use some of the hot water from the geysers to provide central heating in their homes.

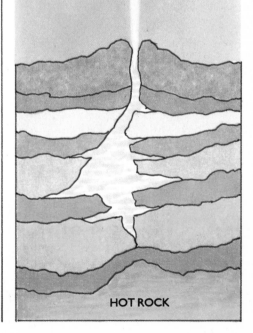

HOT ROCK

THE SUN AND THE EARTH

The Sun is over a million times bigger than the Earth. If the Sun was as big as the dome of St Paul's Cathedral, then the Earth would be just a bit bigger than a football.

The Earth is nearly 150 million km (93 million miles) from the Earth. If the Sun was reduced to the size of a football, then the Earth would be 30m (98ft) distant from it. That is longer than a tennis court, about the same distance as the width of an ice rink or the same length as three double-decker buses bumper to bumper.

The Sun measures 1,392,530km (865,318 miles) across. If it were reduced to the size of a football, then the Earth which measures 12,756km (7,927 miles) across would be no bigger than this dot - smaller than a grape pip!

It takes 8.5 minutes for sunlight to travel from the Sun to the Earth.

The Sun is speeding through space at 250km per second (155 miles per second). That means in one second it has travelled the distance between London and Cardiff or between Edinburgh and Hull.

If you could fly to the Sun in a modern jet aeroplane, it would take you 19 years to get there.

The Earth weighs 5,976 million million tonnes. The Sun is 332,000 times as heavy as the Earth - that is just about 2,000 million million million million tonnes. If the Earth weighed as much as a ping pong ball, the Sun would weigh 830kg (1,830lb), as much as a family car. If the Earth weighed as much as a tennis ball, the Sun would weigh 19 tonnes, more than an excavator.

The Sun is composed mainly of the gas hydrogen. Nuclear reactions at the core of the Sun change hydrogen into helium and generate massive heat. The temperature at the core of the Sun is 15,000,000°C - far hotter than anything we can generate on Earth. The temperature on the surface of the Sun is 6,000°C, hot enough to turn gold, tungsten and every metal on Earth into a gas.

The Sun burns up four million tonnes of hydrogen per second. The energy produced by the Sun in one second would be enough to provide Britain with all the electricity it needs for over 2,500 million years.

Although the Sun is consuming gigantic amounts of fuel every second, it has enough supplies to last it at least another 5,000 million years.

A year and a day.

A year is the amount of time it takes the Earth to orbit the Sun. Other planets orbit the Sun faster or slower than we do, so their years are not the same length as ours.

A day is the amount of time it takes for the Earth to spin round once. Again, other planets spin at different rates and their days are shorter or longer than ours.

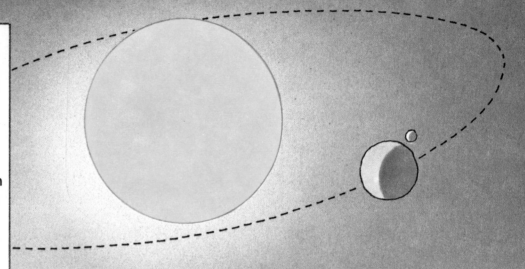

The diameter (the distance through the centre) of the Earth is 12,756km (7,927 miles). The land is only 35 kilometres (22 miles) thick and the land under the oceans is only 6.5 km (4 miles) thick. If the Earth was a balloon 36cm (14inches) across, the depth of the land would be no more than 1mm (0.04inches).

Beneath the crust is molten lava. The temperature rises towards the centre. Scientists think that the temperature of the innermost core is about 6,000°C - the same as on the surface of the Sun and 30 times as hot as a hot oven!

The Earth orbits the Sun at nearly 30km (19 miles) per second. So the next time you are stuck in a traffic jam, just remember that you are actually moving at 108,000kph (67,111mph) - but don't tell the traffic police.

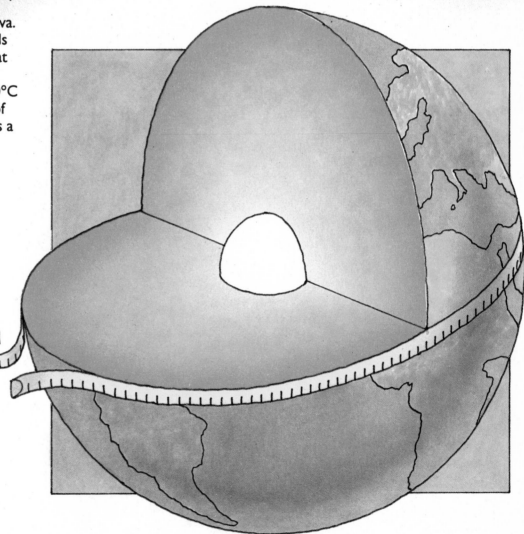

THE MOON

Because there is no air on the Moon there is no wind and no weather. The footprints made by astronauts will last forever unless someone disturbs them.

There is no sound on the Moon because there is no air to carry it.

During the day the Sun warms the Moon - up to 100°C. That is twice as hot as the hottest place on Earth and hot enough to boil water.

At night the temperature plummets far below zero, down to -150°C. That is twice as cold as an Antarctic winter.

The Moon turns on its axis once every 27 days 8 hours. So a day on the Moon lasts for a month!

Astronauts have to wear special suits in space. The suit is a life support system with oxygen, water and a radio. It also keeps out the extreme temperatures.

The hidden side of the Moon.
The Moon orbits the Earth every 27 days 8 hours, the same time it takes to rotate on its axis. This means that the same side of the Moon is always facing the Earth. No-one knew what was on the other side of the Moon until Russia's Luna 3 space probe photographed it in 1959.

The diameter (the distance through the centre) of the Moon is 3,476km (2,160 miles). That is just under a quarter of the length of the Earth's diameter.

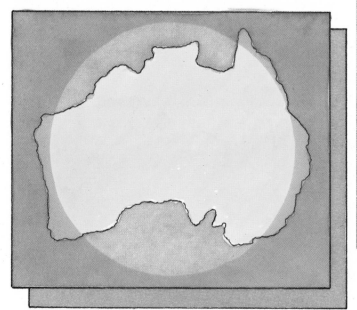

The Earth is nearly 50 times bigger than the Moon, and the Moon is 384,402km (238,867 miles) from the Earth.

If the Earth was reduced to the size of a football, the Moon would be the size of an apple. The distance between them would then be 7m (23ft) - about twice the length of the average sitting room.

If the Earth were reduced to the size of a football, the Sun would be a staggering 2,700m (nearly 3km or 2 miles) away. Can you work out how far away 2 miles is from your home?

Gravity on the Moon is about one sixth that on Earth. If you could jump as far on the Moon as you do on Earth, you could probably jump the same length as Olympic athletes - about 8m (26ft).

You could also jump about 4 or 5m (13-16ft) high - about twice as high as Olympic athletes do on Earth.

The first people to land on the Moon were Neil Armstrong and Edwin Aldrin. On 20 July, 1969 they spent 2½ hours there. No people have landed on the Moon since December 1972. The astronauts left scientific instruments on the surface of the Moon and all their rubbish. The rubbish will remain there for ever.

The surface of the Moon has been bombed by meteorites and asteroids for thousands of millions of years. It is pitted with craters of different sizes. Some are tiny, but the largest, the Orientale Basin, must have been made by a huge meteorite. It is 965 km (600 miles) across. If London was on one side of the crater, Berlin in Germany would be on the other.

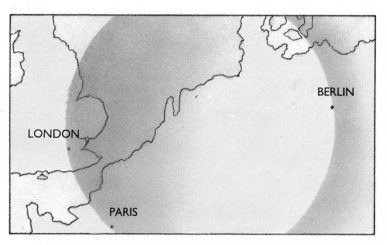

The Moon has huge mountain ranges. The highest mountain peaks are 6,000m (19,686ft) above the ground, two thirds the height of Mount Everest. There is no weather to wear down the Moon's mountains, so they will always remain that high.

If you could fly to the Moon in a modern jet aeroplane it would take you 2 weeks 3 days and 18 hours to get there. But spacecraft travel is much faster and takes only about 4 days.

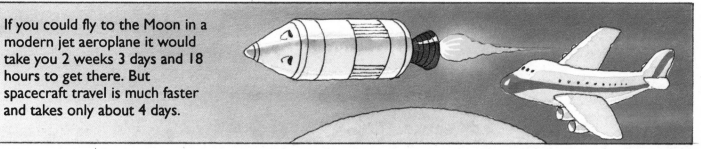

MERCURY, VENUS AND MARS

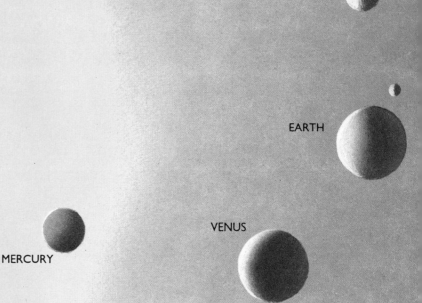

MARS

EARTH

VENUS

MERCURY

Mercury is the closest planet to the Sun. At only 58 million km (36 million miles), it is just over a third of the distance of the Earth from the Sun.

Mercury is the smallest planet of all. Earth is 18 times larger than Mercury. If Earth were reduced to a football, then Mercury would be about the size of a grapefruit. The surface of Mercury is not much bigger than the areas of Africa and Asia together.

Mercury is sunbaked and completely dry. It has no water and no air. Its surface is pitted with craters made by meteorites crashing onto its surface.

The heat is blistering - up to 400°C, which is hot enough to melt lead. The nights are even colder than those on the Moon. The temperature drops to -200°C, nearly cold enough to turn oxygen gas into a liquid.

A day on Mercury lasts for 59 Earth days, but its year lasts only 88 Earth days - less than two Mercury days. On Mercury you would have four birthdays for every one on Earth!

The Sun moves very slowly across Mercury's sky - one of our months pass between sunrise and sunset.

Venus is the hottest planet of all. During the day, the temperature on its surface rises to 460°C (860°F). Venus gets hotter than Mercury even though it is farther from the Sun. This is because it is covered with thick clouds that keep the heat in. The air on Venus is mainly carbon dioxide. The clouds may consist of droplets of sulphuric acid.

Venus is almost the same size as Earth and consists mainly of iron,

nickel and other metals, just like Earth. Its surface is very different, however. Unlike Earth, Venus has no plants and no life. If it had plants, they would have turned much of the carbon dioxide in the air to oxygen.

One day on Venus is longer than a year! The planet takes 243 Earth days to spin on its axis, but only 255 days to orbit the Sun. It spins on its axis in the opposite direction from Earth. If the Sun

could be seen through the thick clouds (which it can't), it would rise in the west and set in the east over 3½ Earth-years later.

Venus is the closest planet to Earth. At times it is as close as 42 million km (26 million miles). If the Earth were reduced to the size of a football, Venus would also be as big as a football, but 755m (2,477ft) away. That is farther than seven football pitches laid end to end.

Mars is farther from the Sun than Earth. Mars is 228 million km (142 million miles) from the Sun. If the distance between the Earth and the Sun was reduced to 2,700m (8,859ft), then Mars would be over 4km (2.5 miles) from the Sun and nearly 1.5km (4,921ft) from Earth.

It is always freezing on Mars. At night the temperature is about -80°C (as cold as an Antarctic winter) and during the day it rises only to about -20°C.

The length of a day on Mars is 24 hours 37 minutes, much the same as that on Earth. But its year is nearly twice as long - 687 Earth-days.

Mars has seasons as we do on Earth. Ice caps at its poles get larger in winter. But the ice is frozen carbon dioxide, not frozen water as on Earth.

There is air and wind on Mars, but we could not breathe in the air as it is mainly carbon dioxide. Much of Mars looks like parts of the Arizona Desert in the United States. The red, sandy ground is covered with rocks. Great storms of dust sometimes blow across the land.

In 1877 an Italian astronomer called Giovanni Schiaparelli spotted what he thought were long straight canals on Mars. This led many people to believe there might be life there. When the American spacecraft Viking landed on Mars in 1976 it made careful tests but found no evidence of life there.

The Earth is about seven times as big as Mars and its diameter is twice as long.

It took Viking a year to reach Mars. It travelled at about 9,000 kph (5,600 mph). It takes about 4 minutes 23 seconds for radio waves and light to reach Mars from Earth. If you were talking to someone on Mars you would have to wait nearly nine minutes for their reply to reach you!

The highest known mountains are on Mars. Olympus Mons is about 27km (88,582ft) high - about three times as high as Mount Everest, Earth's highest mountain.

THE OUTER PLANETS

Jupiter is the largest planet in the solar system. It is as big as all the other planets put together. It is 1,316 times as big as the Earth. If the Earth were the size of a football, Jupiter would be almost as high as your sitting room.

Like the Sun, the planets Jupiter, Saturn, Uranus and Neptune consist mainly of the gas hydrogen. Beneath Jupiter's cloudy surface may be a core of liquid hydrogen.

A gigantic whirlpool.
On the surface of Jupiter is a big red spot, about three times the size of the Earth. The spot is made by a huge whirlpool in Jupiter's gases.

Jupiter has 14 moons, including the largest one of all, Ganymede. Its diameter is less than half that of Earth's, but is bigger than both Mercury and Pluto.

Days go by quickly on Jupiter.
They last just 9 hours 50 minutes. But a year on Jupiter is much longer than on Earth - each one lasts nearly twelve of our years. So there are over 10,000 Jupiter-days in a Jupiter-year - a long time between birthdays!

If the Earth was reduced to the size of a football (diameter 22.6cm or 9in), then Saturn would be as tall as a tall man (2m or 6-7ft) and Uranus, with half the diameter, would be about 1m (3ft). The diameter of Neptune would be 85cm (33in), but Pluto would be only just over 5cm (2in), about the size of a plum.

Rings of dust.

Saturn is circled by huge rings. They are large enough to fit around 400 Earths. The rings are made of space dust and are only a few kilometres thick.

Saturn is very cold. The temperature of its clouds is -180°C. It is so light it could float in water - if there was an ocean big enough to hold it!

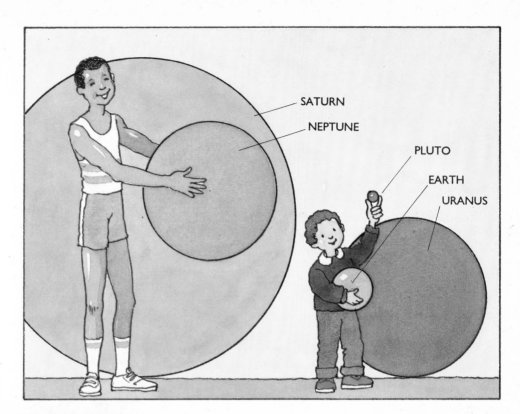

SATURN
NEPTUNE
PLUTO
EARTH
URANUS

Saturn has 18 moons! Some are very small, only about 20km (12 miles) across and cannot be seen from Earth. They were discovered by the Voyager space probes.

Pluto, being the farthest planet from the Sun, takes the longest time to orbit the Sun and so has the longest year - nearly 248 Earth-years. Its day lasts 6 Earth-days and 9 hours, giving it 14,192 Pluto-days in a Pluto-year.

Although Pluto is the farthest planet from the Sun, its orbit sometimes brings it closer to the Sun than Neptune.

Pluto is the farthest planet from the Sun. It is 5,900 million km (3,666 million miles) from it. If the Sun and all its planets were shrunk so that Pluto was the size of a plum, then Pluto would be almost as far from the Sun as Sheffield is from Birmingham. The map shows you where all the outer planets would be on the same scale, if the Sun were in the centre of Birmingham.

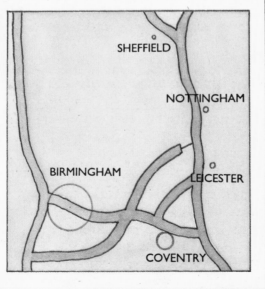

SHEFFIELD
NOTTINGHAM
BIRMINGHAM
LEICESTER
COVENTRY

The spacecraft, Pioneer 10, which was launched in March 1972 took over 14 years to reach the orbit of Pluto. It was travelling around 50,000 kph (31,070mph). If we could travel this speed on land it would take just one minute and half a second to go from London to Inverness.

The temperature on Pluto is -230°C. This is so cold that oxygen could exist only as a solid.

ASTEROIDS, METEORS, COMETS AND U.F.O.S

Scientists have spotted more than 2,000 asteroids. If you were flying a spacecraft to Jupiter, you would really have to watch out for asteroids. There may be as many as hundreds of thousands of asteroids whirling round the Sun in a belt between Mars and Jupiter. The largest of them is Ceres which is just over 1,000km (621 miles) across. This is a bit larger than the distance between Land's End and John O'Groats.

Wandering asteroids.

Icarus, Adonis, Eros and Hidalgo are all wandering asteroids. Instead of orbiting the Sun in the asteroid belt they go both closer to and farther away from the Sun. The path of Eros, Adonis and Icarus cross the path of the Earth. Eros is 23km (14 miles) in diameter. The others are smaller.

Space junk.

The asteroids are solid pieces of rock left over when the planets were formed, 4,600 million years ago. At that time the solar system was a huge cloud of gas and dust. The centre of the cloud came together to form the Sun. It grew big and hot. Other parts of the cloud formed the planets and their moons, or satellites. The pieces left over formed the asteroid belt. Meteoroids and comets still whiz through space, some on a set orbit, others randomly.

Shooting stars.

Have you ever seen a streak of light dart across the night sky, too fast to be a plane, then disappear? These streaks of light are not caused by beings from another world, but by meteoroids - lumps of rock that are sucked into the Earth's atmosphere by gravity, but which burn up long before they hit the ground.

Most meteoroids are tiny - no bigger than a grain of sand.

Some meteoroids are big enough to reach the Earth. Then they are called meteorites. More than 1,000,000 tonnes of meteorites fall on the Earth each year. Most are no more than dust by the time they reach the ground. In fact, next time you come home from a walk, give your coat a shake - you will probably shake off some cosmic dust!

Comets are small chunks of crumbly rock and ice that orbit the Sun, not in a rough circle like the planets, but in an oval path. Sometimes they come close to the Sun. The heat releases clouds of gas and dust which stream behind them like a tail. As the comet gets farther and farther from the Sun the gas and dust freeze back into a huge snowball.

The sight of a comet used to terrify people. They thought it was a sign of impending disaster - the end of the world perhaps.

The appearance of a comet still causes a lot of excitement among scientists and astronomers, but that is because their appearances are so rare.

Halley's comet comes close to the Earth every 76 years. It was last here in 1986 and so will not return until 2062.

The comet Kohoutek will not be seen again for thousands of years. It travels far beyond Pluto and takes 75,000 years to complete each orbit of the Sun.

U.F.O.s.

From time to time, newspapers report strange objects being picked up on radar screens or flying across our skies. What are they? Are they flying saucers from other galaxies, or are they secret military planes that no government wants to admit to? No-one knows for sure, so they are logged as 'unidentified flying objects' or 'U.F.O.s'. Many may be due to clouds, camera flashes or other optical illusions (trick of the light that makes you think something is there when it isn't). We know that no life is possible on the other planets in our solar system, but what about visitors from outer space? Turn the page to see how likely they are.

The largest meteorite to hit the Earth was found in Namibia in 1920. It weighs nearly 60 tonnes and is nearly 3m (10ft) long and about 2.5m (8ft) wide - about the size of a small bedroom.

When the Earth first formed, 4,600 million years ago, it was probably bombarded by meteors, covering it with craters like those on the Moon. Most of these craters have been worn away by wind or rain, or flooded with lava escaping from under the ground.

Large meteorites blast a hole in the ground, like a bomb crater. In the Arizona Desert there is a huge crater, just over 1km (3,280ft) wide. It was made 27,000 years ago by a giant meteorite which must have weighed as much as 2 million tonnes.

An even larger crater was found in Antarctica. It is 240km (149 miles) across and 800m (2,625ft) deep. If this meteorite had hit Britain, Birmingham would be on one side of the crater and Kendal would be on the other, while most of the Midlands and north of England would have been obliterated. But don't worry - this meteorite fell thousands, if not millions, of years ago, long before anyone lived in Britain.

The heaviest meteorite to fall on Britain in the last 350 years weighed 46 kg (101lb). It fell on Leicestershire in 1965.

OUTER SPACE

The Sun is just one star in a galaxy of stars called the Milky Way. There are another 100,000,000,000 stars in the Milky Way and probably another 100,000 million galaxies in the universe.

The nearest star to us is Proxima Centauri. It is 40,850,000,000,000km (25,370,000,000,000 miles) away. If our Sun was reduced to the size of a football, then Pluto, the most distant planet in our solar system, would be 840m (just over half a mile) away, but the nearest star would be 6,000km (3,728 miles) away. That is farther than the distance between London and New York.

The Milky Way spins through space at a staggering 2.1 million kph (1.3 million mph).

Although the diameter of the Sun is a million times bigger than the Earth, it is small compared with some other stars. Betelgeuse, a star in the constellation Orion, is a super-giant, a million times bigger than our Sun and big enough to swallow Venus, Mercury and Earth.

The Dog Star is the brightest star that we can see from Earth. A star starts off as a vast cloud of gas that slowly pulls itself into a huge ball and gets hotter and hotter. The atoms at the centre break down and give out tremendous energy, like our Sun does now. Some stars shine thousands of times as brightly as the Sun, but they do not last long - only a few million years before they exhaust their fuel and die.

Astronomic distances.

Distances in space are so great that astronomers have invented new units to describe them. The most common is a light year and it is the distance that light travels in one year. If you know that light could travel more than five times round the Equator in one second you will realise that one light year is a very long way - 9,500,000,000,000km (5,900,000,000,000 miles) in fact.

Visitors from outer space?

There are so many stars in the universe, many presumably with their own planets, that it is highly probable that life exists on some of them. However, they are so far away it is unlikely that any form of life could reach us here on

Earth. Even if we had a spacecraft that could travel at a million kilometres per hour it would take 4,660 years to reach Proxima Centauri our nearest star, 4.3 light years away. The Milky Way itself is probably 100,000 light years from side to side and most stars are hundreds or thousands of light years away from us.

The North Star is 680 light years away. That means that the light we see at night left the star 680

Red giant.

When a star has used up all its hydrogen fuel, its centre becomes even hotter and the star swells up into a huge red giant. Some red giants are as big as our whole solar system. They would engulf Pluto as well as all the other planets and moons.

White dwarf.

Red giants cool and shrink into white dwarfs. As they get smaller and smaller, even smaller than the Earth, they get denser and denser. Their matter becomes so densely packed, that one teaspoon of it would weigh many tonnes.

Our own Sun has already burned for 5,000 million years. It will probably burn for another 5,000 million before it swells up into a red giant, big enough to swallow Mercury, Venus, Earth and Mars. It will then shrink into a white dwarf before cooling and fading into the darkness of space.

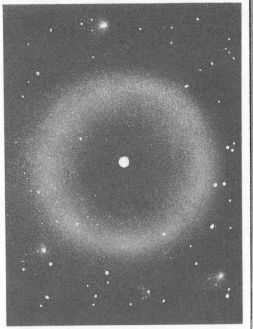

Supernovae.

Instead of becoming red giants, some stars explode. They may shine as brightly as 100 million stars, but they last only for a few days or hours.

years ago - at the end of the Middle Ages when barons lived in castles and fought each other with knights on horseback. If there is intelligent life circling round the North Star that can see us here on Earth, that is what they would see!

How fast will spacecraft travel in the future? Perhaps if they could travel at the speed of light then we could reach other planets spinning around other stars. However, travelling at or near the speed of light brings its own problems. As an object approaches the speed of light it becomes heavier and heavier and time itself slows down. So even if we could send a spaceship to another galaxy, four million years would have passed on Earth before it could return to tell us about it!

Radio signals from outer space.

In 1967 British scientists were puzzled to pick up regular radio signals from a distant object. These were unlike the radio signals usually received from space, and the scientists wondered if another civilisation could be sending them. But as

they studied them further, they realised that they had discovered a new type of star, a pulsar. Scientists think that a pulsar forms when a supernova explodes. It gives out huge amounts of energy, yet may only be 30km (19 miles) across.

Black holes.

Black holes are smaller and denser than pulsars. Scientists think they are massive stars that have collapsed in upon themselves. Their gravity is so strong that nothing, not even light, can escape from them. You cannot see them, even with a telescope, but they suck in anything that comes near them. Don't worry though, the nearest black hole is 8,000 light years away from us!

EXPLORING SPACE

Home telescope

On a clear night in Africa and many other parts of the world you can see thousands of stars, just with your naked eyes. But if you had a telescope with an opening (aperture) about 10cm (4in) across, you could see a million stars.

Telescopes use mirrors and lenses to make distant objects appear larger and closer. The biggest telescope in the world is at Zelenchukskaya in the Caucasus Mountains of Russia. Its aperture is 6m (20ft) wide. Although Mount Palomar in California, U.S.A., has a smaller aperture - 5.1m (17ft) across - it works better. It uses modern technology and is on a better site for observing the sky.

Watching the invisible.

Radio telescopes are designed to detect radio waves that cannot be seen or photographed. These telescopes can pick up radiation from stars that are too far away for optical telescopes to see.

The largest radio telescope is at Arecibo in Puerto Rico. Its aperture is a huge dish 305m (1,000ft) wide. The dish is large enough to hold the whole of Wembley Stadium with room to spare.

The radio telescope at Effelsberg in West Germany is more useful than the Arecibo telescope, which is fixed and can only observe the sky overhead. Although the dish at Effelsberg is smaller - 100m (328ft) across - it can be turned to point anywhere in the sky.

Above is an observatory telescope, below is a radio telescope.

Sputnik.

The first artificial satellite to be launched from Earth was Sputnik 1. It was launched by the Russians in 1957. It measured only 58cm (22.8in) across, not much bigger than a party balloon, but it orbited the Earth every 96 minutes at a speed of 28,000 kph (17,400 mph).

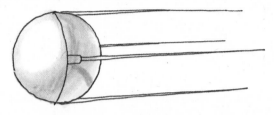

The first person to be launched into space was the Russian cosmonaut, Yuri Gagarin. In 1961, he orbited the Earth once in 108 minutes.

The first people to land on the Moon were American, Neil Armstrong and Edwin Aldrin. In 1969, they spent 2¹/₂ hours on the surface. The last mission to the Moon was in 1972.

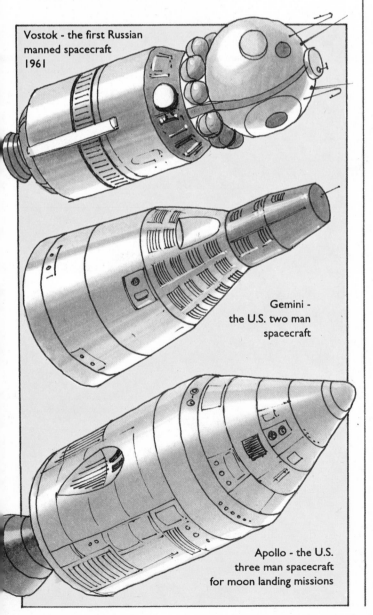

Vostok - the first Russian manned spacecraft 1961

Gemini - the U.S. two man spacecraft

Apollo - the U.S. three man spacecraft for moon landing missions

Living in space.

Astronauts can't drop anything in space or stub their toes. There is no gravity in space, so when they let something go, it simply floats around. If they bump into something it floats off, like apples in a tub of water. They cannot pour a drink because liquid does not flow, it just stays where it is. Astronauts have to suck their drinks through a straw.

Two Russian cosmonauts have spent longer in space than anyone else. Between December 1987 and December 1988, Vladimir Titov and Musa Manarov spent a whole year on the Mir space station. Musa Manarov has now spent a total of 541 days in space, more than anyone else in the world.

Powerful rockets are needed to take a spacecraft out of Earth's gravity. The most powerful rocket to successfully launch an object into space was fired by the Russians in 1987. It carried 105 tonnes up into orbit around the Earth and was nearly 59m (193ft) tall - that's as tall as a 20-storey building.

Long journey ahead.

In 1972, Pioneer 10 was launched from Cape Canaveral in the United States. In 1986, it crossed the orbit of Pluto nearly 6,000 million km (3,728 million miles) from Earth. It will continue to travel through space until it reaches the star Ross 248, which is about 10 light years away - in about 30,000 years time.

The German spacecraft Helios B has travelled faster than any other spacecraft. It orbits the Sun and has reached 250,000 kph (155,350mph).

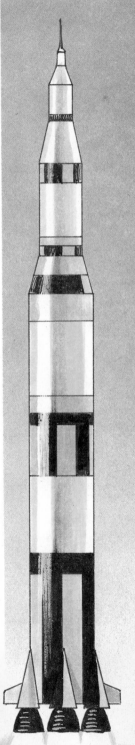

PLANTS AND TREES

The tallest kind of tree in the world is the Australian eucalyptus tree which grows up to 114m (374ft) high, higher than St. Paul's cathedral. If it were possible, you could lean over the balcony on the 38th floor of a high rise block and touch the top leaves of the tree.

Cacti grow in hot, dry places. They have no leaves at all, just spikes to stop animals eating them and thick stems which store water.

The most massive tree in the world is a giant sequoia. It grows in Sequoia National Park in California and is 84m (276ft) tall. Its trunk is about 8m (26ft) in diameter (measured through the centre), large enough to drive a road through if a hole were carved into it.

Arizona's famous bristle-cone pine is young however, compared with some lichens. Scientists have estimated that lichens in the Antarctic may be 10,000 years old. If they are right, these lichens started growing during the Ice Age.

The world's biggest flower is certainly not the prettiest. Rafflesia flowers grow up to a metre across, but they smell of rotting meat. The foul smell attracts flies which pollinate the plant.

Bamboo grows faster than any other plant. It can grow nearly a metre (39.4in) in one day - about the same as you grew in the ten years after you were born.

The leaves of the giant Victorian water lily can be more than 2m (7ft) across, about the same area as a table tennis table. They are strong enough for a child to sit upon without sinking.

The oldest tree in the world is a bristle-cone pine. One in Arizona, United States, is 4,600 years old. It was just a sapling when the pyramids were being built, a tall tree when the ancient Greeks and Persians were battling in the Mediterranean, and was already old when Jesus was born.

No life without plants.

Neither people nor animals can live without plants. They eat them or hunt other animals that feed off plants. Where do plants get their food? They make it themselves from sunlight, water and carbon dioxide in the air. The green leaves and stems are the plant's food-making factory. The waste product - oxygen, escapes into the air - which is just as well because no living thing can survive without oxygen.

OXYGEN

Some plants cannot get all they need from the acid, marshy soil in which they grow, so they catch insects to eat instead! Venus flytraps and pitcher plants lure the insects in with sweet nectar then shut their traps and digest them!

A mushroom is a fruit - it carries spores that blow away in the wind to grow into new plants. But where is the rest of the plant - the leaves, the stem and the flowers? Mushrooms are fungi and they have no flowers. The rest of the plant is underground - it feeds on nutrients of rotting plants and animals.

A fairy ring.

Sometimes toadstools grow in a ring. This is because the plant has used up all the nutrients under the centre of the circle and puts up fruiting bodies (toadstools) at the edge - in a ring.

Rainforests.

Many different kinds of plants and animals live in rainforests. In 10 sq. km (4 sq. miles) of rainforest you could find 1,500 different types of flowers, 750 different types of trees, 400 different types of birds, 150 different kinds of butterflies, 125 different kinds of mammal and 1,000 different kinds of reptiles. All in an area not much bigger than a large town.

The tiny country of Panama has as many different kinds of plants as the whole of Europe, although Europe is 140 times larger than Panama.

Rings of yellowed and burnt-looking grass have led some people to believe that a flying saucer has landed and taken off again, burning the grass with its exhaust. A less exciting explanation is that they are caused by fungi.

Almost everything you eat for breakfast, including Rice Krispies, Cornflakes and Coco-pops, originally came from the rainforests. Many medicines are based on rainforest plants too.

In the last 30 years, two thirds of the rainforest in Central America has been cut down and the land used for cattle-ranching - to produce beef for beefburgers.

Every year 200,000 sq. km (77,220 sq. miles) of tropical forest are destroyed. That is an area nearly as large as Scotland and England together. An area as large as a football pitch is destroyed every second.

INSECTS, SNAILS AND OTHER CREEPY-CRAWLIES

Insects include beetles, flies, butterflies, grasshoppers and many others. There may be as many as 30 million different kinds of insects - more insects than all other kinds of animals put together.

The biggest and heaviest insects are beetles. The male Goliath beetle can be as long as 15cm (6in). It may weigh up to 100g (3½oz) as heavy as a standard Mars Bar.

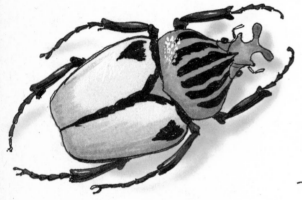

The longest insect is a kind of African stick insect. It can grow up to 40cm (16in) long.

Millipede means 'a thousand feet', but so far no millipede has been found to have more than 710 legs.

A mayfly lives for only one day.

Many insects have an amazing sense of smell. Flies find their food by following - not their noses, but their antennae. Some beetles have very fancy antennae.

It is very difficult to swat a fly. One reason is that flies can see in 4,000 different directions at once! Their eyes are made up of that number of different facets (or lenses).

Ever wished you could be a fly and walk upside down on the ceiling? To do so, you would need to have sticky pads under your feet, like a fly's.

Butterfly wings have beautiful coloured patterns. They are made up of tiny scales which overlap like the tiles on a roof.

Each spring, Painted Lady butterflies fly 5,000km (3,107 miles) as they migrate from North Africa or Asia to Europe.

Grasshoppers can leap about 75cm (30in), about 20 times the length of their body. If you could do as well, you could jump 30m (98ft), over three times as far as the world's best Olympic long jumpers.

Stick insect, approximately life-size.

Insects have no voice. The sounds they make are all produced by their wings or legs. Grasshoppers 'sing' by rubbing their legs against a rough patch on their wings.

A grasshopper's ears are on its legs.

A tiny flea can jump a distance of 33cm (13in) in one leap. It jumps high as well - nearly 20cm (8in) up into the air. A flea can jump 130 times its own height. If you could do that you could jump about 200m (656ft) high. You could easily leap over St Paul's Cathedral (111m or 364ft), but not quite Canary Wharf (228m or 748ft).

A snail's eyes are at the ends of its horns.

A snail can sleep for up to three years without waking up.

Worms have no eyes at all, not surprising since they spend most of their time burrowing through the soil. Their skin, however, is sensitive to light, so you could say they see through their skin.

One type of Southern African worm is almost 7m (23ft) long. If it were drawn life-size with its tail at the beginning of this page, its head would not appear for another 31 pages!

Locusts sometimes gather together in huge swarms. The skies turn dark as they fly overhead and they consume every green leaf and blade of grass in sight. In 1899 it was estimated that a swarm around the area of the Red Sea covered 5,200 sq. km (2,008 sq. miles) - an area half the size of Northern Ireland.

Insects can increase in number very quickly. A queen termite can lay 8,000 eggs a day, every day for years.

Termites build their nests in huge mounds many times taller than themselves. If people lived in huge buildings equivalent to a termite's nest, they would be over 4,000m (13,124ft) high - half the size of Everest.

Ants are very strong. They can pull things 300 times heavier than themselves and lift things 50 times their own weight. Even the strongest men cannot lift much more than twice their own body weight.

You can tell a spider from an insect because spiders have eight legs. The largest spider of all is a bird-eating spider from South America. Its body is about 7.5cm (3in) long, but it measures more than 25cm (10in) long from one hairy foot to the other.

The most famous poisonous spider is the Black Widow spider, but there are several other spiders that are just as poisonous. The most toxic is probably a Brazilian wandering spider that likes to hide inside houses, in shoes and other dark corners. Luckily, the Brazilians have a very good antidote to its bite.

Most spiders are our friends as they catch flies and other insects. There are millions of them in Britain. In an area of countryside about the size of an ice rink you could find up to a million spiders. If you could weigh all the insects consumed by spiders in England and Wales in one year you would find they weighed the same as all the people who live there.

Silk from a spider's web is stronger than steel thread of the same thickness.

FROGS, SNAKES, CROCODILES AND OTHER REPTILES

The largest frog is the Goliath frog. It lives in tropical Africa and its body may be as long as 36cm (14in). With its legs stretched out, it is more than double that length.

Frogs have very long tongues that are attached to the front of their mouths. They stick them out to catch insects so fast you would be lucky to see them.

Frogs can jump 5.3m (17ft 7in) - more than half as far as the best Olympic athletes. If you could jump as well as a frog, you could jump at least 150m (492ft) - one and a half times the length of a football pitch.

Frogs do not have waterproof skins like we have. In fact they take in both air and water through their skins. To stop all the moisture from inside their bodies escaping, frogs have to keep their skin damp.

Some frogs live high in the trees of the rainforest. There is enough moisture dripping from the leaves to keep their skin damp. They have special suction pads under their feet to help them climb the slippery bark.

Golden poison dart frogs in Colombia, South America, are the most poisonous frogs of all. Each frog has enough poison in its skin to kill 1,500 people. Why are they called poison dart frogs? Because the local Indians used the poison to make lethal darts.

The longest snakes are the anacondas of South America and the reticulated python from S.E. Asia. Both can grow nearly 9m (30ft) long. If one coiled itself around the outer edge of a table tennis table its mouth would touch the end of its tail.

A snake's jaws are joined by loose ligaments. This means that snakes can open their mouths very wide - wide enough to swallow a meal two or three times the size of their own heads. One reticulated python even managed to swallow a bear weighing 91kg (200lb).

Pythons and anacondas kill their prey by coiling themselves round it and strangling it to death. Other snakes kill their victims by injecting them with poison from their fangs.

The poisonous fangs of the Gaboon vipers in tropical Africa can be up to 5cm (2in) long.

The most poisonous snakes live in Australia. A bite from the Australian taipan can kill a person in a few minutes.

A snake changes its skin several times a year. As it slides out of the old skin a new one is ready underneath.

Warming up.

Reptiles cannot make their own body heat like birds and mammals. Instead reptiles warm their bodies in the sunshine. At night or when it gets colder, they slow down and go to sleep until it gets warmer again. Lizards dart in and out of the shade to keep themselves at the right temperature.

Battle for colour.

Male Green anoles are usually grey. But when two rivals fight, their skin changes colour. You can easily tell who has won the battle because the winner is bright green. The loser is yellow!

The shingle-backed lizard of Australia is slow and clumsy, but it has a hidden weapon to scare away its enemies. It sticks out its blue tongue and hisses loudly.

It is hard to spot a chameleon until it moves. The colour of a chameleon's skin changes to fit in with the colour of its surroundings.

The largest lizard is the Komodo monitor of S.E. Asia. It looks like a dragon and can grow up to 3m (10ft) long - as long as a Mini.

When the frilled lizard is attacked, it spreads out a fold of skin around its neck to make it look big and ferocious. It also hisses loudly.

The largest reptile of all is the Estuarine crocodile of S.E. Asia. It can grow up to 6m (20ft) long. It would make a few waves in the swimming pool!

If you lived in Miami you might well find an alligator in your swimming pool. The marshes where they used to live have been drained, so the alligators have moved into the swimming pools instead.

Crocodiles have strange toothbrushes. Plovers use their long beaks to peck bits of food and parasites from between the crocodiles' teeth.

Probably the first thing you notice about a crocodile, or alligator, is its teeth, but baby alligators are quite at home among them! The mother carries her babies in her mouth to take them in and out of the water.

Crocodiles are in much greater danger from people than we are from them. Hunters kill them for their skins which are made into handbags and suitcases. So many crocodiles and alligators have been killed that they have disappeared from many parts of Africa. It is now illegal to kill crocodiles or alligators.

BIRDS

Ostriches are the biggest birds. They grow up to 2.5m (8ft) tall. They can't fly, but they can run fast - up to 50kph (31mph).

The smallest bird is the bee hummingbird. It lives in Cuba and measures less than 5cm (2in) from the tip of its long beak to the end of its tail. It weighs only 2g (0.07oz), about as heavy as half a teaspoon of water. It would take fourteen bee hummingbirds to balance a hen's egg.

Approximately life-size.

The bee hummingbird's eggs are only about 1cm (1/2in) long. An ostrich egg on the other hand, is usually about 18cm (7in) long. It would take over 4,000 hummingbird eggs to equal the weight of one ostrich egg.

Hummingbird egg actual size.

Most birds build a nest in which the female lays her eggs then sits on them until they hatch. A finch has to wait only 12 days for her eggs to hatch, but a royal albatross has to sit for a staggering 79 days.

Some birds do it differently!

When an emperor penguin lays an egg she immediately and carefully passes it to her mate who tucks it under a fold of skin between his belly and his feet. The female then goes off to find food, leaving the male with the egg for 63 days. Emperor penguins live in the Antarctic so the poor male has to withstand freezing cold blizzards, standing in one spot.

Cuckoos pass on the difficult business of hatching eggs and feeding the young to other birds. The female looks for a nest full of eggs and pushes one of them out. She then lays her egg in its place. When the baby cuckoo is born, it too pushes out its rivals. Eventually the baby cuckoo is the only one in the nest and the foster parents continue to work hard to feed it, even though it may grow to be many times bigger than themselves.

A wandering albatross measures 3.6m (11ft 9ins) from wing tip to wing tip. It is wider than the smallest aeroplane whose wingspan is only 2.18m (7ft 2ins).

Swifts are the fastest birds and they can travel faster across ground than any other animal. They fly up to 160kph (100mph) and could overtake all the traffic on the motorway.

Swifts can stay in the air for two to three years at a time. They feed, drink, mate and even sleep while airborne.

Birds of prey have very good eyesight. As they hover many metres above the ground they can detect the slightest movement of a mouse in the grass below. It is thought that a Peregrine falcon can see a pigeon up to 8km (5 miles) away.

When an owl, eagle or other bird of prey has spotted its target, it swoops down and grasps its prey in its claws. Eagles can even carry off young lambs and other animals weighing as much as 9kg (20lb).

Birds have no teeth so they swallow their food whole. Owls cannot digest the bones and fur of their prey, so they regurgitate them in the form of a pellet with other undigested bits of food.

Hens swallow grit and small stones. The stones help to grind up the food in their stomachs.

BEARS, APES, ELEPHANTS AND OTHER BIG MAMMALS

Grizzly bears are the biggest and fiercest of all bears. They grow up to 3m (10ft) tall - too big to get through your front door! They weigh up to 750kg (1,653lb) - as much as eight heavy men. They are easily irritated and can knock over a human with just one swipe of a paw.

Many bears sleep right through the winter. They eat enough food in the summer to give themselves a thick layer of fat, then they dig a hole in the ground in autumn and sleep there until spring.

Pandas are not bears - or are they? Scientists are still not sure. Some say they are raccoons, but all agree that these attractive animals are in danger of dying out

altogether. Their natural home is China but the bamboo which is a large part of their diet is being cut down to make way for fields and villages. Only about 1,000 still live in the wild and those in captivity do not breed easily.

Noisy eaters.
Sloth bears love to eat termites. They break into their nests and

suck them out with long tongues. They slurp so loudly they can be heard up to 200m (656ft) away!

Chimpanzees are clever animals and often resemble human beings. You can tell from their expressions how they are feeling and they use instruments to feed themselves. For example they use leaves to scoop water from a stream, and to eat termites they push a stick into the middle of the nest, wait for the termites to crawl on and then they lick them off.

Gentle giants.
The largest apes are gorillas. They grow nearly 2m (6½ft) tall, but are about twice as heavy as a person of the same height. They are very strong but not fierce. Gorillas are vegetarians - they eat fruit, leaves, twigs and even bark.

The most agile apes.
Gibbons are the acrobats of the jungle. They swing from tree to tree in the forests of S.E. Asia where they live. From time to time, they stop to pick a juicy fruit, leaf or shoot to eat.

Sloths have very uneventful lives. They spend almost all their time hanging upside down from the branch of a tree. Occasionally they reach out an arm and pluck a leaf to eat. They spend so much time upside down, their fur grows from their tummy to their back.

Big cats.

Tigers are the biggest of all big cats. They grow up to 3m (10ft) long from nose to tail. They are up to 1m (3ft) high at the shoulder.

All cats have beautiful fur and all, except lions, have been hunted close to extinction. Jaguars, leopards, panthers, cheetahs, ocelots, tigers, lynx and caracal are now all protected species - it is illegal to kill them without a permit.

Cats' bodies are well suited to hunting. As well as being lithe, they have good eyesight, sharp teeth and claws, and can move swiftly and silently up to their prey. Baby tigers learn how to hunt by pouncing on their mothers' swinging tails.

Cheetahs are the fastest of all land animals. They can run at 112kmh (70mph), but for only about 300m (984ft). So if you ever find yourself being chased by a cheetah along the motorway, don't worry - just keep driving and the cheetah will give up.

Watch out for the prong-horned antelope. Its fastest speed is only

96kph (60mph), but it can keep going for much farther than the cheetah.

Giraffes may reach up to 5.5m (18ft) tall. They can reach the juiciest new leaves at the tops of the trees and look down on all the other animals from their great height. But surprisingly they have no more bones in their necks than you do and their legs are thin and wobbly. When they need to bend to drink, they must do so very carefully!

African elephants are massive animals. They grow up to 3.5m (12 ft) high and weigh up to 7 tonnes. It would take more than eighty people to balance the weight of a single elephant.

An elephant uses its trunk to smell, to lift things, to spray itself with water and dust, and to make a noise like a trumpet. Its trunk is strong enough to lift a heavy load, and sensitive enough to pick up a single peanut. It can even untie a rope.

Baby elephants suck their trunk for comfort, just like small children suck their thumbs.

Elephants look after each other. When one is sick or dying, the other elephants try to help it to its feet. Baby elephants are looked after by the females in the group.

Camels are well suited for life in the desert. As well as having a store of fat in their humps, they have long eyelashes to keep the sand out of their eyes. They can close their nostrils to stop the dirt getting in and their broad feet stop them sinking into the sand.

Red kangaroos can bound over the Australian outback at more than 48kph (30mph). They can jump over 12m (40ft) in one bound - about 3m (10ft) farther than Olympic athletes.

A Red kangaroo may grow to be about 2.6m (8ft 6ins) long, but when it is born it is no more than 2cm (3/4in) long. It crawls through its mother's fur and into her pouch where it stays until it is big enough to leave.

SEA MAMMALS

Sea mammals.
Whales, dolphins, seals and walruses are mammals like us. They cannot breathe oxygen from the water as fish do, but must come to the surface to breathe in air. They can hold their breath for much longer than we can - some for an hour or more. Whales breathe out through a blowhole in the top of their heads - then a misty plume rises high into the air.

Like all mammals, sea mammals do not lay eggs but give birth to babies that the mother feeds with her own milk. Seals and walruses come onto land to give birth, but whales and dolphins give birth at sea. The newborn calf must be nuzzled to the surface to take its first breath of air.

The blue whale is the biggest animal that has ever lived. They grow up to 30m (98ft) long - as long as three buses end to end and much larger than an elephant or giraffe.

Blue whales are also the world's heaviest animals. They weigh up to 190 tonnes - as much as 2,000 heavy men or 52 buses.

Blue whales feed on some of the world's smallest creatures - krill, a kind of small shrimp. They have no teeth. Instead they take in huge gulps of water and sieve the food through their baleen plates, swallowing up to 1,000kg (2,205lbs) of food at each meal.

As humpback whales migrate to warmer water, they sing. The song gradually changes as they move along, but as they set off on the return journey back to the Poles they take up the song where they left off.

Humpback whales scratch themselves against undersea rocks to scrape off the barnacles that cling to their skin.

Dolphins are very intelligent creatures. For some reason they seem to like humans and will often play with swimmers in the sea.

A big baby.

A newborn blue whale calf is about 7m (23ft) long and weighs up to 3 tonnes. By the time it is a year old it weighs about 26 tonnes, which means that it puts on about 2.5kg (5½lbs) every hour!

Blue whales spend the summer feeding in the icy waters of the Antarctic or Arctic. Then they swim about 15,000km (nearly 10,000 miles) to tropical waters near the Equator to breed. But there is very little food for them in the tropics. They have to live off the fat they put on in the summer.

Dolphin language.

Dolphins are a kind of whale. They use a range of high-pitched clicks, groans and whistles to communicate with each other. Dolphins are short-sighted and they also use these sounds to help them find their way. Like bats they can tell from the returning echoes how close they are to submerged mountains, rocks and other things.

A dolphin nicknamed Pelorus Jack, used to swim with ships through part of Cook Strait in New Zealand. He would meet a ship at one end of the strait and escort it part of the way. Then he waited for a ship sailing the other way. Pelorus Jack did this for 24 years before someone shot at him in 1912.

Seals and walruses spend part of their lives on land. The fins they use for swimming become legs for walking.

Walruses use their long tusks to dig out shellfish from the seabed. They also use them to haul themselves out of the water onto the ice.

Killer whales hunt in packs. They attack penguins, seals, fish and even other whales. They eat them with their sharp teeth. But do not worry, killer whales do not attack human beings.

Killer whales can swim up to 55kph (34mph).

Sperm whales dive deep to catch giant squid, octopuses and other prey. They dive up to a kilometre below the surface and can stay underwater for 1½ hours.

OTHER SEA CREATURES

The largest shark is the whale shark which can grow up to 15-18m (50-60ft) long - longer than five Minis bumper to bumper. The whale shark is quite harmless, except perhaps to the tiny plankton it feeds on.

The most deadly shark is the Great White Shark. It has attacked many swimmers in the tropical seas in which it lives.

Sharks have a very good sense of smell. They use it to track their victims.

Have you ever had rock salmon from a fish and chip shop? It is not a kind of salmon, but a small shark, often known as dogfish because it scavenges the seabed.

The electric eel of South America kills its prey by stunning it with an electric shock. It can discharge 500 volts of electricity into its victim, enough to kill a person.

Squid and octopus move through the water by a kind of jet propulsion. They push water out of their bodies, so propelling themselves forward.

Squid and octopus squirt out inky-coloured water when they are attacked. Octopuses, believe it or not, are closely related to snails!

Giant squid are over 13m (43ft) long. Of this their long tentacles measure 9m (30ft) - almost as long as a bus.

A sailfish can swim up to 96kph (60mph). At this speed it could cross the English Channel in just 20 minutes, three times as fast as the cross-channel ferries!

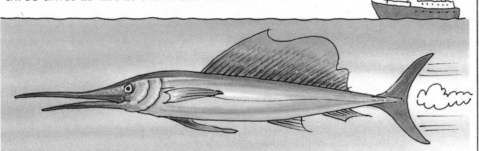

Flying fish can move at 64km/h (40mph) - faster than many ships. They leap out of the water and glide on outstretched fins for over 100m before dropping back into the water over half a minute later.

Remora fish hitch a ride on larger fish, such as sharks. They have a large oval sucker with which they attach themselves to their host. Then nothing can dislodge them until they swim forward. In the meantime they share the host's food and eat smaller fish.

Archer fish shoot down their prey with a well aimed spit. They live in freshwater and feed on insects that they dislodge from overhanging twigs and leaves.

Not all jellyfish can sting you, but the Portuguese man o' war certainly can. Its tentacles are about 10m (33ft) long. They are lined with stings as poisonous as the sting of a cobra.

Only oysters can make pearls inside their bodies. If a tiny grain gets inside its shell, the oyster coats it with layer upon layer of shell and makes it into a pearl.

Oysters and other shellfish feed by opening their shells just a little. As the water flows through, fine hairs around the opening trap microscopic plants and animals and pass them along to the shellfish's mouth.

Unlike other crabs, the hermit crab does not make its own hard shell. Instead it finds an empty shell discarded by another shellfish and moves in. As the hermit crab grows bigger, it moves from one shell to another.

Moving house.

As shellfish grow, their shells grow with them. As a nautilus gets bigger it adds a whole new chamber and moves into it. It carries all the old out-grown chambers behind it, but makes

good use of them. When it wants to sink lower in the sea, it fills up the empty chambers with water, and when it wants to float up again it fills them with gas.

If a starfish loses a limb, it simply grows another one! Its limbs are covered with powerful suckers. It can attach itself to a shellfish and force open its shell wide enough to feed on the creature inside.

Sea horses drift along with the current. When they want to stop, they hook their tails around a piece of seaweed. Sea horse fathers look after the young. He keeps the eggs in a pouch in his belly until they are ready to hatch.

EXTINCT ANIMALS

Dinosaurs are the largest animals that have ever lived on land. They roamed the Earth for about 160 million years, but died out 65 million years ago. The first people did not appear on Earth for another 64 million years and have, so far, lived for only a fraction of the time that dinosaurs did.

The largest dinosaur was Brachiosaurus. It was nearly 24m (79ft) long and its head reached 17m (56ft) above the ground to munch the leaves on which it fed. It could have looked over the top of a house and, if it had stood in the gardens, its tail would have been four houses away from its nose.

Brachiosaurus would certainly have crushed a few flowers. It weighed up to 51 tonnes - as heavy as 250 Sumo wrestlers.

Diplodocus was even longer than Brachiosaurus. It measured 27m (89ft) from the tip of its nose to the end of its tail, nearly as long as three buses, bumper to bumper.

Diplodocus's tail was so far from its brain, it is just possible that you could have stood on its tail and run away before the message reached the dinosaur's brain. But it would have been wiser not to try it! Diplodocus had such a small brain in its head that scientists think it may have had a kind of second brain lower down its spine to control the back part of its body. If that was so, one swipe of its tail would have knocked you out!

Tyrannosaurus Rex was the largest meat-eating dinosaur. It was 16m (52ft) long and stood up to 6m (20ft) high. Its huge jaws were full of dagger-like teeth 15cm (6in) long. But Tyrannosaurus Rex may not have been as ferocious as it looked. Its front legs were so small and weak, it would not have been much of a fighter. Most likely it preyed on old or weak dinosaurs, or scavenged the left-overs of other dinosaurs' prey.

The skulls of bone-headed dinosaurs were up to 23cm (9in) thick. They probably used their skulls like battering rams, charging each other in combat. And what was all this armour protecting? Underneath it lay a small brain.

Most dinosaurs had small brains compared with their body size. Stegosaurus's brain was no bigger than a walnut.

Not all dinosaurs were huge. Compsognathus was only about 75cm (2ft 6ins) long, about the size of a large modern chicken.

The largest flying reptile was Quetzalcoatlus. Its wings were made by a layer of skin stretched between thin struts of bones. They measured 11m (36ft) across, making Quetzalcoatlus about the same size as a Spitfire - the famous fighter plane of World War II.

The largest prehistoric mammal was a kind of hornless rhino called Paracerathium. It lived 35 million years ago and was 11m (36ft) long - almost as tall as a giraffe, but much heavier. At 34 tonnes, it was five times as heavy as an elephant.

Several huge mammoths have been found perfectly preserved in the Arctic ice a million years after they died. Mammoths had long, hairy coats and tusks up to 5m (16ft) - as long as a large sitting room.

Like most of today's reptiles, dinosaurs laid eggs and hatched out their young. Instead of sitting on the eggs they probably covered the nest with leaves which kept the eggs warm as they decomposed. The largest fossil eggs belonged to Hypselosaurus. They were each 30cm (12in) long and 25.5 cm (10in) across - bigger than a soccer ball.

Ankylosaurs were like living tanks. Their bodies were covered with thick plates of bone, studded with knobs and spikes. At the end of their tails were spiky clubs, very useful for knocking over their enemies.

Eohippus was a prehistoric ancestor of today's horse. But Eohippus was no bigger than a modern pet cat.

WHAT'S THE TIME?

It all depends where in the world you are. When it's breakfast time (8am) in New York, it is lunchtime (1pm) in London, tea time (at 4pm) in Moscow, dinnertime (at 8pm) in Jakarta, Indonesia and bedtime (10pm) in Tokyo, Japan. In Wellington it is 1 o'clock in the morning and most people are asleep. As the Earth spins, the Sun is always rising somewhere in the world and always setting somewhere else.

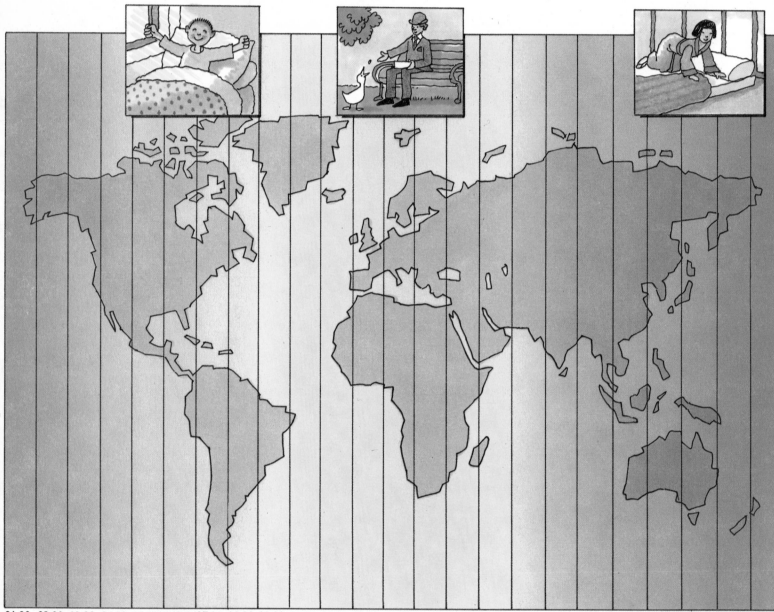

01.00 02.00 03.00 04.00 05.00 06.00 07.00 08.00 09.00 10.00 11.00 12.00 13.00 14.00 15.00 16.00 17.00 18.00 19.00 20.00 21.00 22.00 23.00 24.00

As astronauts orbit the Earth they may see the Sun rise and set up to eight times between breakfast (8am) and supper (8pm).

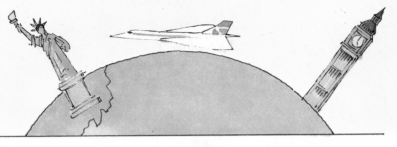

If you flew from London to New York by Concorde, the flight would take only three hours. But the time difference between the two cities is 5 hours, so if the plane took off at 5 o'clock in the afternoon, London time, it will land in New York at 3 o'clock in the afternoon!

If you have a clock that doesn't work it will at least show the correct time twice a day. But if you have a clock that loses a minute a day, it will show the correct time every 720 days, just ten days less than two years!

In the Middle Ages an hour in the summer was longer than an hour in the winter! The time between sunrise and sunset was divided into twelve equal 'hours', however long or short daytime was.

The Earth was formed about 4,600 million years ago. The first simple living cells may have appeared in the oceans about 1,000 million years later. Life slowly became more complicated, until 500 million years ago the seas were teeming with ancient shellfish and other sea creatures. Fishes did not appear for over another 100 million years and dinosaurs for another 300 million years. Our own ancestors date back to about 1 million years ago.

It is difficult to grasp the length of time involved, even in a million years. But suppose that time since the Earth formed (4,600 million years) is represented by one year and the Earth formed on the 1st of January. Then the first simple cells appeared around the 29th March, but the first fishes were not seen until the 27th of November. The first dinosaurs began to roam the Earth on December 15th and did not die out until the 26th of December. Ape-people appeared at about 6.15pm on the last day of the year and Christ was born just 14 seconds before midnight.

4,600 MILLION YEARS AGO
The Earth formed from clouds of gases and dust.

3,800 MILLION YEARS AGO
The great rains came, cooled the Earth and formed the seas.

500 MILLION YEARS AGO

400 MILLION YEARS AGO

280 MILLION YEARS AGO

1-60 MILLION YEARS AGO

THE HUMAN BODY

All adults except giants and dwarfs, are between 140cm (4ft 7in) and 200cm (6ft 7in) tall. In America and Europe, the average woman is 160cm (5ft 3in) and the average man is 173cm (5ft 8in).

A few people have too much or too little growth hormone. The tallest man accurately measured was Robert Wadlow, an American. He was 272cm (8ft 11in) tall. Although he was 22 years old when he died in 1940, he was still growing. The tallest woman was Chinese. She measured 247cm (8ft 1in) when she died in 1982.

The average Briton eats each year 78kg (172lb) of potatoes, 26kg (57lb) sugar, 208 eggs, 150 loaves of bread and 50 packets of biscuits and much else as well.

An American showman known as General Tom Thumb was only 102cm (3ft 4in) tall when he died in 1885 at the age of 47.

The average weight for men is 76kg (168lb). The average weight for women is 64.5kg (142lb). A scientist has calculated that American people carry more than two million tonnes of excess fat between them.

The heaviest person ever recorded was an American man. When he died in 1983 he weighed over 363kg (800lb), but it is calculated that a few years earlier he had weighed over 635kg (1400lb).

You can survive without a stomach but you cannot live without your liver! It monitors the amount of digested food in your blood to make sure the body gets only the right foods. It extracts poisons and stores extra sugars and fat. If part of your liver is removed the rest will take over and grow until the missing part is replaced.

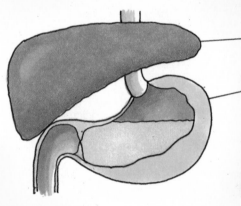

Our food has a long slow journey through the digestive system. When you eat a meal, most of the food is churned around in your stomach for between two and four hours before passing into the long coiled tube of your intestines to be digested. It takes between 15 and 25 hours for the discarded food to reach the end of this journey and several days before the last of your meal finally disappears.

Human stomachs allow us to eat a lot, but they are small when compared with those of some animals:
Human stomach holds about 1.5 litres (2.5 pints)
A large dog's stomach holds about 3 litres (5 pints)

A pig's stomach holds about 8 litres (14 pints)
A horse can consume up to 18 litres (4 gallons)
But a cow can consume up to 180 litres (40 gallons) - as much as 80 big plastic containers of milk!

You have about 656 different muscles. Exercise increases their size and strength but does not add to their number. Even something as straight forward as walking involves 200 different muscles. You use about 40 muscles when you frown, but only 15 when you smile - so keep smiling!

The fastest muscles are those that blink your eyelids. They allow you to blink up to 200 times a minute. You normally blink without thinking - in fact it is hard not to blink and impossible to manage for as long as a minute.

Muscles account for 4 tenths of your weight, but much of your body, including muscles, is water. Apart from blood, spit, urine and other bodily fluids, the solid parts of your body contain so much water that, in total, 7 tenths of you is water.

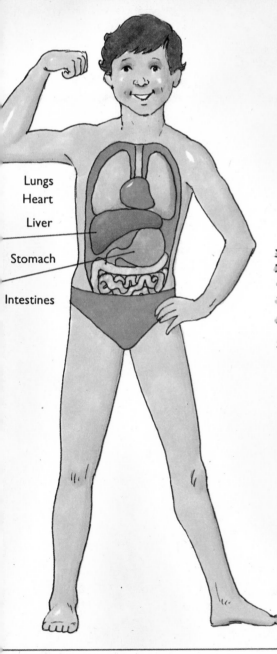

Lungs
Heart
Liver
Stomach
Intestines

Your heart is a pump that sends blood to your lungs And to every part of your body except your hair and nails. The arteries that leave your heart are the widest blood vessels, but most blood vessels are so narrow you can hardly see them. Altogether an adult has 100,000km (62,140 miles) of blood vessels. If they were laid end to end they would stretch two and half times round the Equator.

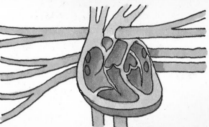

When you are resting, your heart beats about 70-80 times a minute. So it beats about 100,000 times a day, and if you live to be 70 it will have to beat nearly 3,000 million times without stopping.

In Medieval times the liver was thought to be the most important organ in the body. It was called the seat of life and people thought that if you were angry, sad, good-humoured, calm or peevish, it depended on your liver.

An adult man makes about 1.5 litres (2.5 pints) of spit every 24 hours. Saliva contains an antiseptic which helps to kill germs.

You lose between 1 and 2 litres (1.75 and 3.5 pints) of urine each day. You lose less in hot weather, but more if you drink a lot.

Although urine is a poison, it contains no germs. It is often used in emergencies - in the middle of a battle for instance - as an antiseptic for cleaning wounds.

I'm sure that you know when you cut yourself you bleed. The bleeding stops when the blood in the wound clots. But did you know that applying a spider's web to the wound can make it clot faster. It is probably not a good idea because the web may have trapped dirt and germs.

In the past, people used to think that bleeding helped to fight disease and calmed the nerves. At first, blood letting, as it was called, was done by cutting blood vessels, then by employing leeches. These little creatures were scooped from rivers and

lakes and attached to the skin. Each one could suck 14g (½ oz) of blood. One doctor alone is said to have been responsible for the letting of millions of litres of French blood, more than was lost in the Napoleonic wars which were going on at the same time.

Adults take in about 0.5 litres (just under half a pint) of air with every breath. So every day each person needs about 15,000 litres (530 cu ft) of air - about the amount contained in a baby's bedroom. In a lifetime each person breathes in about 400,000 cu metres (14 million cu ft) of air - twice the volume of St Paul's Cathedral. It is likely that the air you breathe has already been breathed in and out several times since the world began.

Although you breathe air and swallow food through your mouth, a flap of skin at the back of your throat, called the epiglottis, closes off the wind pipe when you swallow. This

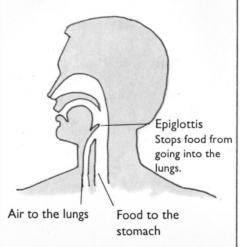

Epiglottis
Stops food from going into the lungs.

Air to the lungs   Food to the stomach

stops food going into your lungs, but sometimes the system fails. If food 'goes down the wrong way', you choke. A famous engineer called Isambard Kingdom Brunel once swallowed half a sovereign,

worse still, it went down 'the wrong way'. He asked to be hung upside-down and hit on the back, but the sovereign remained stuck. His windpipe was cut but the sovereign could not be found. Six weeks later he tried the upside-down treatment once again and luckily the sovereign fell back into his mouth.

If all the tubes and little round air sacs in your lungs were laid out flat they would cover a tennis court!

When you are doing something quiet, like reading this book, you breathe about 15 times a minute, but when you are rushing about you breathe much faster. If you live to be 75, you will have breathed no less than 600 million times.

Your skin is a stretchy waterproof surface that covers your entire body. Without it, your insides would dry out and dirt and germs would get in. It is tough enough to withstand most scratches and bangs, yet it is only 2mm (0.08in) thick - about as thick as the cover of this book - and is packed full of sweat glands, hair roots, blood vessels and nerves.

There are more than 100 sweat glands for each square centimetre of skin (about 650 per square inch). Each day you lose between 0.5-1 litre (1-1¾ pints) of sweat, probably without realising you are sweating at all. Tennis players on Centre Court on a hot day certainly know they are sweating. In fact they lose up to 1.7 litres (3 pints) an hour. No wonder they need a drink.

The thickest skin - 3mm (0.12 in) is on the soles of your feet. Your eyelids on the other hand are only 1mm (0.04in) thick.

Lips and fingertips are among the most sensitive parts of your body. So is your tongue. Pieces of food stuck between your teeth seem huge to your tongue, when they are actually very small.

You shed a complete layer of skin every month. The top layer consists of hard, horny dead cells and they flake off all the time. Most of the dust in your house is actually dead skin! New skin is forming all the time below the old skin.

Hair and nails are also made of dead cells. They are not fed by blood or nerves. That is why you can cut them without it hurting.

Hair grows from the hair root in the skin. The hair root is fed by blood and nerves, so if you pull your hair it certainly hurts. Have you noticed too, that pulling just one hair hurts more than pulling a handful. That is because the pull is spread between many different hairs.

Your hair grows about 2.3mm (0.09in) a week, that is about 12cm (4.75in) a year. In a lifetime you produce about 8.5m (28ft) of new hair, but whether you have it cut or not, you will not be able to grow it that long.

You lose between 30 and 60 hairs every day, but don't worry, that still leaves you with about 100,000 and new hairs are growing all the time. Each hair lasts from one to six years before the hair root withers and the hair drops out. After 3 or 4 months rest, the hair root starts to produce a new hair. This means that not even quick-growing hair can grow much longer than 75-90cm (30-35ins) - just long enough to sit on. Strangely, a woman in Sweden managed to grow her hair 3.2 metres (10ft 6in) long.

AIR TRAVEL

The first plane to take off, fly and land using engine power was built by two bicycle manufacturers in Ohio, U.S.A. It was called the *Flyer* and was built and flown by the Wright brothers, Orville and Wilbur, in 1902. It flew only 37 metres (121 feet), but it realised a dream that had existed since the ancient Greeks - to fly like a bird.

Previous attempts to build a flying machine had failed, partly because they tried so hard to imitate a bird. In the 15th century, Leonardo da Vinci had designed a plane with flapping wings, and in the year before the Wrights' historic flight many other attempts to build mechanical flapping wings failed.

Pioneering flights.

Aeroplanes developed quickly. Just seven years after the Wrights' first flight, Louis Bleriot flew 37km (23 miles) across the English Channel from France to England. Ten years later, in 1919, John Alcock and Arthur Brown flew non-stop across the Atlantic Ocean. It took them 16 hours.

Until 1917, aeroplanes were made out of wood. Towards the end of the First World War, wood ran out, so engineers tried metal instead and found it was better.

Airspeeds.

The fastest aircraft ever was the Lockheed SR-714A reconnaissance plane. In 1976, it flew just under 3,530kph (2,193mph).

3,530 Kph

Concorde is the fastest passenger plane. It can cruise at up to 2,333kph (1,450mph) and

2,333 Kph

has flown from New York to London in less than three hours.

The first successful attempt to fly was made in a paper balloon! It was made in 1783 by the Montgolfier brothers in Paris. They filled it with hot air and slung a basket below it. The first passengers were a duck, a sheep and a cockerel! When they came to no harm, two daring Frenchmen - Francois de Rozier and the Marquis of d'Arlandes - tried it too and became the world's first aeronauts.

In the 1920s many airships were built. They were basically huge balloons filled with hydrogen and powered with hydrogen and powered by an engine. They crossed the Atlantic and it looked set to become the most popular way to fly. But hydrogen catches fire very easily and several airships came to a disastrous end. People refused to fly in them and turned to aeroplanes instead.

The Hindenberg was the longest airship built before the Second World War. It was 246.7m (809ft 4in) long - longer than 2½ football pitches laid end to end - but it carried only 75 passengers (plus 25 crew).

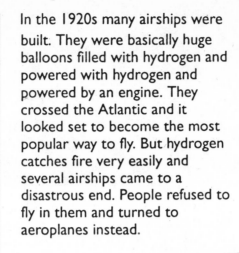

The Wrights' *Flyer*'s first flight was less than the length of a Boeing 747.

The first plane to fly faster than the speed of sound was the Bell X-1. In 1947 it flew at 1,078kph (670mph) just 12kph faster than sound.

1,078 Kph

68.3 Kph

When Bleriot crossed the English Channel in 1909 his average airspeed was 68.7kph (42.7mph).

The Bell X-1 was powered by rockets, not jet engines. Another rocket plane the X-15A-2, launched in mid-air in 1967, attained the fastest speed of all, 7,274 kph (4520mph).

SHIPS

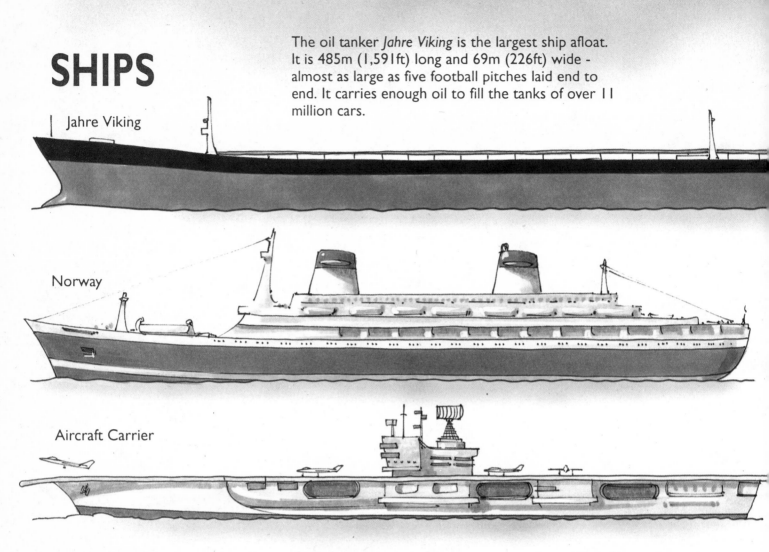

Jahre Viking

The oil tanker *Jahre Viking* is the largest ship afloat. It is 485m (1,591ft) long and 69m (226ft) wide - almost as large as five football pitches laid end to end. It carries enough oil to fill the tanks of over 11 million cars.

Norway

Aircraft Carrier

The biggest passenger liner is the Norwegian ship *Norway*, launched in 1961. It is 315m (1,033ft) long and carries 2,400 people. If all the passengers arrived at the ship by train, it would take 30 railway coaches to carry them all - nearly four full train loads!

Today the biggest warships are aircraft carriers. The United States Navy's Nimitz class are 333m (1,092ft) long. The flight deck is nearly 2 hectares (5.5 acres) - as large as ten ice rinks and nearly as large as three football pitches.

Nelson's ship *Victory* led the defeat of the French Navy at the Battle of Trafalgar in 1805. It was only 57m (187ft) long, but it took the wood of over 2000 oak trees to build it.

Roman fighting ships were called 'galleys'. They were about 71m (233ft) long.

Robin Knox-Johnson's yacht *Suhaili* was only 9.9m (32ft) long, yet he sailed it single-handed around the world.

Remarkable voyages.

The first Europeans to reach the American continent were probably the Vikings. They sailed via Iceland and Greenland.

In 1519, Magellan set out from Spain to sail round the world. It took him just two weeks short of three years.

In 1968, Robin Knox-Johnson set sail from Falmouth in Cornwall to sail on his own round the world. It took him 312 days sailing west to east.

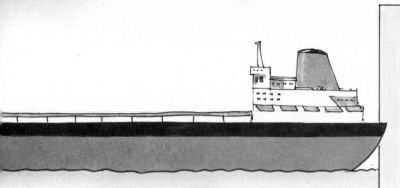

The deepest dive ever made by a submarine is 6,000m (19,686ft), achieved by the U.S. Navy's *Sea Cliff* in 1985. But in 1960, a bathyscaph descended nearly to the bottom of the Marianas Trench in the Pacific Ocean - a depth of 10,915m (35,812ft).

Submarines have sailed right under the Arctic Icecap. Nuclear subs do not burn air and can stay underwater for many weeks, as long as their fuel and stores last. The longest known stay under water is 111 days - just under 16 weeks.

Before aeroplanes became the cheapest and quickest way to cross the Atlantic, ships used to compete for the 'Blue Riband', the award given for the fastest crossing. The current record was set in 1952 by the liner *United States,* which crossed at an average speed of 66kph (41mph). However, a sailfish can swim half as fast again as the *United States*.

United States

The fastest destroyer was the French *Le Terrible*. In 1935 it reached 83kph (52mph). This is faster than the Nimitz aircraft carriers which reach only 56kph (35mph).

Just as steamships were taking to the seas about 100 years ago, sailing ships used to race each other from China to London, hoping to be the first to land their cargo of tea. On one occasion the *Cutty Sark* averaged 33kph (21mph) for its 110 day journey.

Cutty Sark

Mystery at sea.
In 1872 the crew of the *Dei Gratia* spotted a sailing ship out of control. When they boarded the ship called *Mary Celeste* they found half-eaten food on the table but no-one on board. There was no sign of a fight and to this day no-one knows what happened to the crew.

The fastest speed ever reached on water is 556kph (345mph). It was achieved by Kenneth Warby in his hydroplane *Spirit of Australia,* in Australia in 1977.

ROAD TRAVEL

Thrust 2
The world official land speed record holder.

The fastest cars are rocket-powered cars, especially built to break the speed record. They are not powered by a petrol engine, but by a rocket. In 1979 *Budweiser Rocket* travelled at 1,190kph (739mph), faster than the speed of sound. Were the *Budweiser Rocket* able to travel at that speed up the M1 and M6 from London to Glasgow it would complete the 640km (397 miles) journey in just 32.5 minutes.

In 1983 the rocket car, *Thrust 2,* travelled for one mile at a staggering 1,019kph (633mph) and holds the official land speed record.

The fastest motor race was won by a Ford Thunderbird. At Daytona in Florida in 1987 the driver, Bill Elliott, averaged 318kph (198mph) over the 50-mile race.

The Lamborghini Countach is probably the fastest road car. It can go up to 288kph (179mph) - well over the legal speed limit in Britain.

The biggest car ever built is the Bugatti Royale (also known as the *Golden Bugatti*). It is 6.7m (22ft) long - two thirds as long as a London bus. Unlike London buses, they are very rare. The first was made in 1927 and only six were built.

The most popular car ever made is the Volkswagon Beetle. Over 21 million have been sold since the first one was made in Germany in 1938. They are still being produced in Mexico.

Not as rare as the Duesenberg SSJ however. They date from 1934, but only two were made. Each is now worth over £1 million - cheap compared with the £6,400,000 paid by a Swedish man for a 1962 Ferrari 250 GTO in 1990.

£1,000,000

£6,400,000

The most economical car on fuel is the Citroen AX 14DTR and the Daihatsu Charade Diesel Turbo. Both can do 27km per litre (78 miles per gallon) driving at a steady 90kph (56mph). But even better fuel saving may be to come. The Japanese have built an experimental car which does

2,269km on one litre (6,409miles on a gallon). This car could make the round trip from London to Edinburgh and back to London almost eight times on a single gallon of fuel.

Even a small amount of fuel causes pollution. The cleanest car will be one powered by energy or fuel from the sun. Experimental solar-powered cars have already been built and reached speeds of up to 78kph (48mph).

Early cars also had to travel on untarred roads. Clouds of dust were thrown up and covered everything within reach of the road.

Early cars were seen as frightening, noisy and dirty. Until 1896 in Britain, cars were not allowed to exceed walking pace and a red flag, carried in front, warned pedestrians and horses of their approach.

Cars quickly became popular - too popular perhaps. Nearly 35 million new cars were made in 1991 alone. Most cities are choked with traffic jams. The longest traffic jam ever was not in a city but on the East/West German border. In April 1990, for the first time for over 40 years, East Germans were free to enter West Germany and there was a queue of 1.5 million cars!

The longest traffic jam in Britain involved only 50,000 cars and coaches, but in 1987 it stretched for 64 km (40 miles) along the M6 in Lancashire.

Britain's biggest car park is at the National Exhibition Centre in Birmingham. It holds 15,000 cars and 200 coaches. If you go there, don't forget where you parked!

Most cars drive around more than half empty with only one or two people in them. How much clearer the roads would be if more people travelled by bus. An average double decker bus holds 72 people. That is as much as 48 cars!

The largest buses are in the Middle East. They are 23m (75ft) long - more than twice as long as a London bus - and hold 187 people. They are articulated like trucks to help them turn corners.

The largest land vehicle ever built was that used to carry the Saturn V rockets to their launch pad in Cape Canaveral, Florida. This huge vehicle is 40m (131ft) long and nearly 35m (115ft) wide. Over 200 cars could park in the space it takes up!

Bicycles cause no pollution either. The fastest speed reached on one is 105kph (65mph) in 1986 in California.

The first bicycles were velocipedes, but they had no pedals. You had to push yourself along with your feet on the ground.

Penny-farthings look like the worst design idea ever. They may have been difficult to ride, but their main advantage was to keep the rider clear of mud that splashed up from the untarred roads.

Australia has the longest trucks of all. Several trailers are joined together to make a truck train, pulled by just one cab. Truck trains travel on special roads, carrying goods from one side of the country to the other.

RAILWAYS

The fastest speed ever achieved on land was by an unmanned rocket sled specially built by the Americans. In 1982, it slid along a rail at 9,851 kph (6,121mph). At that speed it could cover the journey between London and Glasgow in less than 4 minutes.

The French railways TGV is the fastest passenger train. It can travel at up to 515kph (320mph) although its usual speed is around 210kph (130mph). The letters TGV stand for Train à Grande Vitesse (train at great speed).

The fastest journey made by steam train was one made by *Mallard* in 1938. It pulled seven coaches at 202kph (126mph) for just over 400m (437 yards).

The first passenger train was designed and sometimes driven by George Stephenson. His engine the *Rocket* first ran between Stockton and Darlington on 27 September 1825. *Rocket* never went faster than 21.5kph (13.5mph), but it is said that many people fainted with fear.

In 1968 a train just over 6km (4 miles) long left West Virginia for Ohio. Three engines in the front pulled 500 coal wagons with the help of three more engines pushing from the rear. Twenty one years later an even longer train was assembled in South Africa. It was 7km (4.5 miles) long and consisted of

The longest railway tunnel in the world is the Seikan rail tunnel which links the Japanese islands of Honshu and Hokkaido. It is 54km (33miles) long and is bored under the Tsugaru Strait. The idea was to bring the rural people of Hokkaido in reach of the big cities of the main island, Honshu, but so far, few people have chosen to use it.

Let's hope the tunnel under the English channel fares better. This 50km (31mile) tunnel links south-east England with northern France.

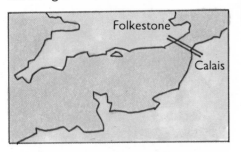

London's Underground railway is the largest system of its kind. It has nearly 170km (105miles) of tunnels.

The busiest underground system is the Moscow Metro. Up to 3,300 million passengers use it each year. The huge underground stations were also designed as nuclear fall-out shelters to protect the people of Moscow.

The longest straight line in the world is the 478km (nearly 300 miles) stretch of railway track across the Nullarbor Plain in Australia.

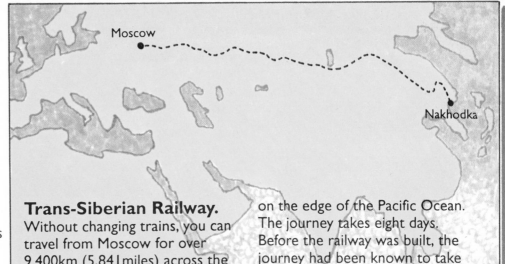

Trans-Siberian Railway.
Without changing trains, you can travel from Moscow for over 9,400km (5,841miles) across the wastes of Siberia to Nakhodka on the edge of the Pacific Ocean. The journey takes eight days. Before the railway was built, the journey had been known to take two years.

The Orient Express.
Before the days of cheap air flights, the Orient Express was the best way to travel from London through Vienna to Istanbul in Turkey. The train still runs with the original exotic carriages and passengers dressed for the occasion.

Around The World...
Jules Verne wrote a book *Around The World In 80 Days*. Magellan, the first person to travel around the world, took 2 years, 354 days. In 1990, six drivers and two cars drove over 40,000km (25,000 miles) round the world in just under 40 days. The first airmen to fly right round the world flew for 371 hours in 1924. In 1988 a Boeing 747 with 141 passengers reduced the time to just under 37 hours. But this is slow compared with spacecraft which orbit the Earth in just 81 minutes.

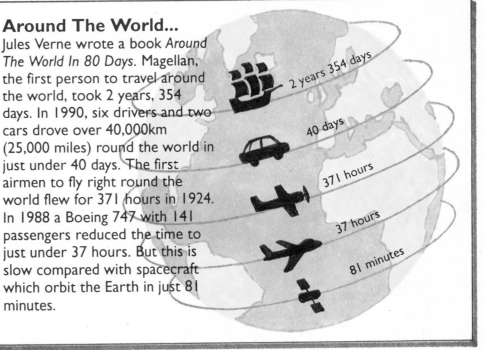

662 wagons pulled by 16 engines, scattered along its length. The front of the American train is shown below. If the whole train was shown it would run back through the book to page 2.

UNDER THE MICROSCOPE

Microscopes make things look bigger. The stronger the microscope, the more it magnifies and the more you can see.

This dot is about the size of a flea.

This is the same flea magnified ten times.

To see bacteria you would need to magnify them 10,000 times. Now you can see how different bacteria vary in appearance.
To see viruses - the kind of germs that give you a cold - you have to magnify them 100,000 times.
Viruses cannot live on their own. They can live and multiply only inside other cells.

Bacteria x 10,000

Virus x 100,000

To see atoms you have to magnify them 10 million times. These are atoms of iron and sulphur. Each larger iron atom has two smaller sulphur atoms attached to it, making a molecule of iron sulphide.

In warm, moist conditions, bacteria can multiply very quickly. They multiply by simply splitting into two identical cells. *Escherichia coli* is a bacterium which lives in the human gut. Each bacterium can split in two every 15 minutes. So an ebacteria can increase to 40,000,000,000,000,000,000,000,000,000 in just 24 hours. Luckily for us, our bodies' own defences kill off most bacteria as they form.

Cells are the building blocks of life. A human baby grows from one cell to 2,000 million cells in just nine months.

Cells are tiny, too small to be seen except under a microscope - except for the female egg cell. Each egg cell is about half the size of a grain of salt.

A cubic centimetre of blood, that is enough to fill a cube the size below, contains 5 million red blood cells, 5,000 to 10,000 white blood cells and a quarter of a million platelets. Red blood cells carry oxygen around the body. White blood cells fight disease and platelets help blood to clot when you cut yourself.

Red blood cells live for one to four months, but in that time each red cell travels round your body up to 172,000 times. New red blood cells are made in your bone marrow. The red jelly at the centre of some bones. To keep you healthy your bone marrow makes around 5 million new red blood cells every second.

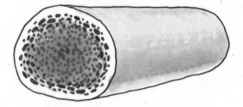

Bacteria are the smallest things that can live on their own. A litre (1.75 pints) of ordinary city air contains about a million bacteria. Luckily, most of them are harmless.

The smallest bit of any substance is called a molecule. Molecules are made up of atoms of different substances. They are too small to be seen without a microscope. It takes 33,000,000,000,000,000,000,000 molecules of water to fill one cubic centimetre.

Water is made up of hydrogen atoms and oxygen atoms joined together. Hydrogen can exist on its own, but it would take 2,000,000 atoms of hydrogen to cover the head of a pin.

Although objects seem to us to be solid, they are mostly made up of space, just as most of the universe with all its stars is mostly space. This is why radio waves can pass through what appear to us to be solid roofs and walls.

Cubic centimetre

Red blood cells x 100

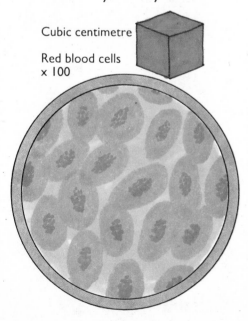

An atom consists of a nucleus with electrons spinning round it, rather like the planets spinning round the Sun. All electrons are the same and are all very, very small. The Sun is as many times heavier than a water melon as a water melon is heavier than an electron.

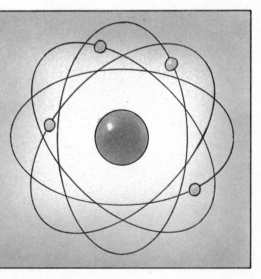

PEOPLE AROUND THE WORLD

The population of the world is increasing by about 250,000 people every day. This means that a city the size of Newcastle or Liverpool is added every two days.

At the last count in 1992, there were about 5,500,000,000 people altogether, and it is estimated that there will be over 6000 million people by the year 2000.

The country with the most people is China. It has over 1,160 million people. If they were all acrobats and were able to stand in groups of three on each other's shoulders, this human column would reach up through the air and into space as far as the Moon.

If everyone in the world held hands they would form a vast chain 3,700,000km (2,300,000 miles) long - long enough to stretch round the world more than 90 times.

However, it is also possible that everyone in the world, standing shoulder to shoulder could fit onto the island of Anglesey and certainly into an area the size of South Yorkshire.

The smallest country in the world is the Vatican City. This small area in Rome is governed by the Pope and not by the Italian government. It covers only 44 hectares (120 acres) - about 60 football pitches - and only 750 people live there.

Mongolia is the emptiest country in the world. Although it is more than six times bigger than the United Kingdom, only 2 million people live there. In case you are thinking of emigrating you should know that it is a high, cold desert.

The largest country in the world is the CIS (formerly the Soviet Union) shown in red. It covers 17,000,000 sq km (6,564,000 sq miles) nearly one eighth of all the land. It is more than twice as big as Canada, the second largest country. When it is breakfast time in Moscow in the west, it is tea time in Vladivostock in the east.

The richest countries in the world are Bahrain and Qatar. These small countries control large oil wells which make so much money none of the inhabitants pays income tax.

About one in every five people in the world live in China, but India is catching up. By the year 2050, the population of India is expected to have grown from 900 million to 1,600 million.

In the Stone Age, about 10,000 years ago, 100 people may have lived in the whole of the area below. Today more than 100 people live in the tiny square in the centre.

Switzerland is the world's most peaceful nation. The last time they fought in a war was in 1815.

In the past 100 years there have been more people living on Earth than in all of the preceding 10,000 years.

The only continent not owned by any country is Antarctica. All countries have agreed to preserve Antarctica as a wilderness and not to mine its stores of minerals. No-one lives there permanently, although scientists brave the freezing temperatures for months at a time.

For thousands of years the human population increased only very slowly. 10,000 years ago there were scarcely more than 5 million people in the world - less than the population of London today. At the time of Christ, 2,000 years ago, there were probably between 200-300 million people. By 1650, this had increased only to 500 million. Then 150 years ago, world population began to increase rapidly. Around 1850 there were 1,000 million people and they had doubled in number by about 1930. Since 1950, the population has mushroomed.

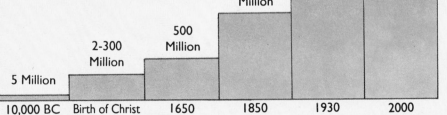

| 6000 Million |
| 2000 Million |
| 1000 Million |
| 500 Million |
| 2-300 Million |
| 5 Million |

| 10,000 BC | Birth of Christ | 1650 | 1850 | 1930 | 2000 |

PEOPLE AROUND THE WORLD

The Union Jack is three flags in one. The red on white cross of St. George of England lies over the red on white cross of St. Patrick of Ireland and both overlay the white on blue cross of St. Andrew of Scotland. Only Wales is unrepresented.

The flag for the Republic of Ireland consists of a green stripe for the Roman Catholics and an orange stripe for the Protestants, separated by a white stripe of peace.

India's flag has the same colours as Ireland's, but here the orange stripe represents Hindus and the green stripe Muslims. The white stripe of peace which separates them has the wheel of Ashoka for Buddhists.

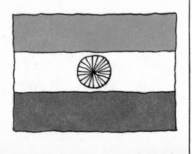

More people speak Chinese than any other language. About 1,000 million people speak Mandarin Chinese, not only in China itself but in Hong Kong, Taiwan and any other country where Chinese people have settled, such as Britain, Australia and the United States. The symbols below mean 'How are you?' in Chinese.

你好嗎

'Kung fu' in Chinese means 'play time'.

English is the most widely spoken language. Apart from 300 million or more people who speak it as their first language, another 1,000 million can also speak English.

Inuits (Eskimos) are surrounded by snow for most of the year. This is reflected in their language which has 20 different words to describe snow. The Arabic language has even more words for camel.

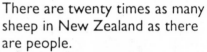

There are twenty times as many sheep in New Zealand as there are people.

In Tibet it is good manners to stick your tongue out at guests. If you invite an Arab family to dine with you, do not be surprised if they burp loudly after the meal. They are only being polite and showing you how much they enjoyed the food.

There are more dogs in Paris than there are children.

In Tokyo there is a restaurant for dogs.

In some restaurants in China you can choose a snake which is cooked for you there and then.

At midnight on New Year's Eve, many Spanish people eat 12 grapes. They hope it will bring them good luck in the year to come.

Japanese do not shake hands when they meet or say goodbye. They bow instead.

The song 'Happy Birthday to you' is the world's most popular song. It is sung in almost every country.

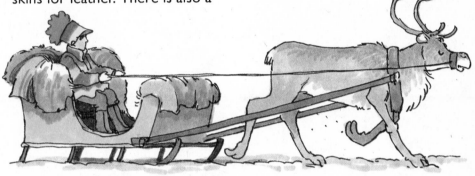

People in Lapland really do use reindeer to pull their sledges. They also drink reindeer milk and eat their meat. They use their skins for leather. There is also a place called Santa's Grotto, but it is only open in summer and around Christmas - when there are most tourists!

At some Greek weddings, guests do not give presents to the bride and groom, but pin money onto the bride's dress.

The Bible is the world's best-selling book. Over 2,600,000,000 copies have been sold in over 300 languages.

Yucatan is a place in Mexico. When the Spanish explorers first arrived there they asked what the place was called. The Indians did not understand Spanish and replied 'Yucatan', which means "What do you want?"

Paduang women of Burma wear many brass rings around their necks. They make their necks longer, a sign of beauty and protect them from being savaged in the neck by tigers.

CITIES

The oldest city in the world is Jericho. People have lived there for over 9,000 years. There are many ancient cities in Iraq and Syria. Babylon was already a beautiful city, famous for its hanging gardens, when people in Europe were still living in caves.

Mohenjo-Daro, in what is now Pakistan, had piped water and drains over 4,000 years ago. Many European cities had to wait until about 150 years ago before they were so well supplied.

The largest city in the world is Mexico City with a population of over 20 million. In 1975 about 10 million people lived there, and in 1950 the population was less than 3 million. A small teaspoon holds 100 grains of rice. If you count out one grain of rice for each person in Mexico City you would need 5 supermarket trolleys to carry all the rice.

New York was first called 'New Amsterdam' by Dutch colonists after their principal city in Holland. In 1664, it was taken by the English and renamed 'New York' after James, Duke of York, brother of King Charles II.

Each day, people in New York use 3,800 million litres (1,000 million U.S. gallons) of water. They also consume nearly 2.5 million kg (6 million lbs) of vegetables, 1.25 million kg (3 million lbs) of meat and 108 million eggs.

There are more Italians in New York than in Rome.

The city of St. Petersburg has changed its name several times in the last hundred years. After the Russian Revolution of 1917, it changed its name from St. Petersburg to Leningrad. When Lenin died and Stalin ruled in the Soviet Union, it was called Stalingrad. Then Stalin died and it became Leningrad again, until, in the 1990s, Communism in Russia was overthrown and the city once again became St. Petersburg.

There is virtually no risk of fire breaking out in La Paz, the capital of Bolivia. This South American city is nearly 4,000 metres (13,124 ft) above sea level, and at that altitude there is scarcely enough oxygen for anything to burn. La Paz does have a fire service however - just in case!

La Paz means 'peace' in Spanish, but Bolivia has been anything but peaceful. There have been over 100 revolutions there, more than any country in the world.

The telephone system in Cairo was so bad that in the 1970s few people had telephones and there were no directories. Businessmen used to fly to Athens to telephone other countries.

It is said that Melbourne in Australia is the second largest Greek city after Athens. (Athens is the capital of Greece).

In Canada, no-one could agree on the choice of the capital city. Should it be Quebec, Kingston, Montreal or Toronto? Queen Victoria was asked to decide in 1858 and she chose Ottawa. The other cities were not amused!

In the City of London there were no roads at all - only streets! The roads through Greater London became streets when they reach the City.

Venice is famous for its beautiful buildings and many canals, yet Birmingham has more canals than Venice.

Los Angeles has more cars than people. It has been estimated that one third of the land area is taken up by roads, and one third by space for parked cars, leaving only one third for the people to live and work.

Los Angeles means 'the angels', but the citizens are no angels! The city has one of the highest crime rates in North America.

In the United States, there are more guns than people.

Tokyo, capital of Japan, is one of the world's biggest and most overcrowded cities. Men known as 'pushers' are employed to pack people onto the city's trains.

BUILDINGS, BRIDGES AND STATUES

The Taj Mahal, one of the most beautiful buildings in the world, is in fact an enormous tomb. Shah Jahan loved his wife so much he had it built for her when she died. He too was buried there when he died in 1666.

The tallest skyscraper in the world is Sears Tower in Chicago. It has 110 storeys and is 443m (1,453ft) high. It has over 16,000 windows and more than 100 lifts. Sears Tower is almost twice as tall as Canary Wharf, the tallest skyscraper in the UK, and nearly six times as tall as Big Ben in London.

The Great Pyramid of Cheops was built over 4,000 years ago and is still standing today. It is so massive, four cathedrals the size of St. Paul's in London could be built inside it. The pyramids were built solely as tombs for the Pharaohs.

The biggest statue in the world is a figure of a woman and is called Motherland. It is 82m (269ft) high, about 50 times larger than life-size. It was erected on a hill near the Russian town of Volgograd to remind people how the city of Stalingrad successfully held out against Hitler's army during the Second World War.

The Statue of Liberty stands on an island in New York harbour. It is twenty times larger than life-size and is a symbol of freedom and the United States. But it was made in France and given to the Americans in 1884. You can climb up the spiral stairs inside the statue to a platform in the crown on top of her head.

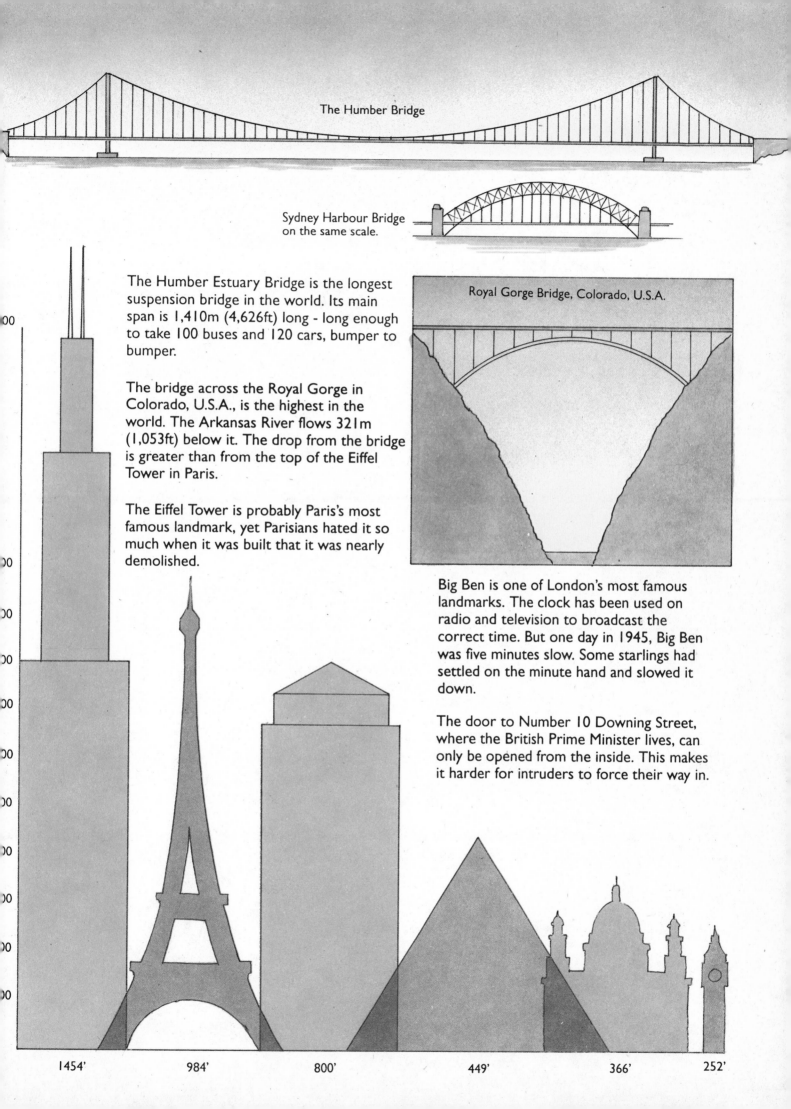

The Humber Bridge

Sydney Harbour Bridge on the same scale.

The Humber Estuary Bridge is the longest suspension bridge in the world. Its main span is 1,410m (4,626ft) long - long enough to take 100 buses and 120 cars, bumper to bumper.

The bridge across the Royal Gorge in Colorado, U.S.A., is the highest in the world. The Arkansas River flows 321m (1,053ft) below it. The drop from the bridge is greater than from the top of the Eiffel Tower in Paris.

The Eiffel Tower is probably Paris's most famous landmark, yet Parisians hated it so much when it was built that it was nearly demolished.

Royal Gorge Bridge, Colorado, U.S.A.

Big Ben is one of London's most famous landmarks. The clock has been used on radio and television to broadcast the correct time. But one day in 1945, Big Ben was five minutes slow. Some starlings had settled on the minute hand and slowed it down.

The door to Number 10 Downing Street, where the British Prime Minister lives, can only be opened from the inside. This makes it harder for intruders to force their way in.

1454'   984'   800'   449'   366'   252'

FOOD, GOLD AND MANUFACTURED GOODS

Diamonds are one of the most expensive jewels in the world, but did you know they consist of carbon - the same basic material as coal?

When the Spanish conquistadors reached South America in the 1500s, they found that gold was the most common metal used by the Inca Indians. Because they had no iron, they made knifes and combs and other ordinary things from gold.

Even in Medieval times, many people wanted to get rich quick. Alchemists tried everything they could to change common substances into gold. In the process, one of them accidentally discovered gunpowder (although the Chinese had been using gunpowder in fireworks for centuries).

There is about 200 times more gold buried in the sea than has been mined from the land. If it were all mined, gold would lose its high value.

At one time, the states of America were colonies of Britain. In 1773 the colonists decided to break away from Britain and form an independent country. The main cause of the quarrel between them? Tea! The Americans did not see why they should pay tax on it. A group disguised as Indians dumped huge quantities of tea into Boston Harbour. This became known as 'the Boston tea party'.

In Wales seaweed is used to make a kind of bread called laver bread.

When potatoes were first brought to Europe in the 1500s, only rich people could afford to eat them.

In China the nests of swiftlets are made into bird's nest soup and considered a rare treat.

Stainless steel does not rust and is used for cutlery, teapots and many other things. It was discovered by accident in 1913. Pieces of steel that had been used for experiments were thrown away, but then someone noticed that while most of the pieces rusted, a few stayed bright and shiny. These pieces were retrieved and examined and became the first pieces of stainless steel.

A North American Indian called George Crum invented potato crisps.

Coca-Cola originated in the United States and is now sold in over 150 countries. More than 90 million bottles of Coke are drunk every day.

Aspirin is made from the bark of willow trees, but it is not a good idea to simply chew some willow bark next time you have a headache!

Adults can survive without food for four weeks or longer, but will die without water after two days.

Much of the food you eat is really water. Cucumber is 96% water, milk is nearly 90% water, potato and steak are over 70% water. Cheese at 40% and bread at 35% are more solid.

When tobacco was first brought to England in the 1600s, King James I wrote a booklet to dissuade people from using it. Unfortunately no-one took any notice. Had James I succeeded, millions of people would have led much healthier lives.

GREEN FACTS

Each person in Britain uses about 50,000 litres (11,000 gallons) of water each year. About one third of this is flushed down the toilet and a further 40% is used for washing and bathing. If we had our water delivered, each of us would need more than four tankers a year.

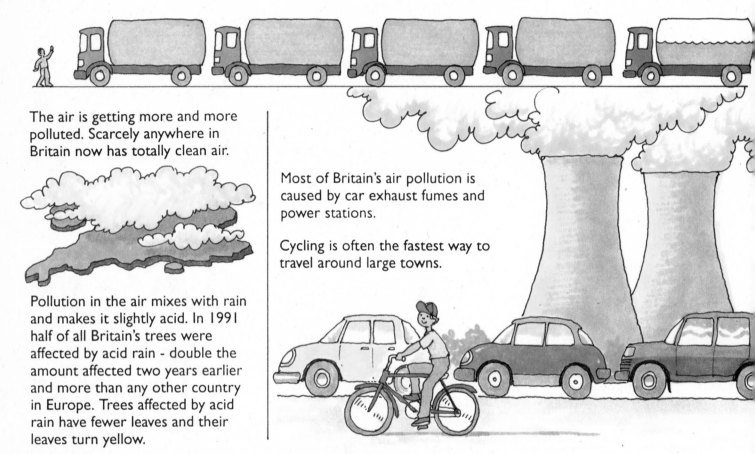

The air is getting more and more polluted. Scarcely anywhere in Britain now has totally clean air.

Pollution in the air mixes with rain and makes it slightly acid. In 1991 half of all Britain's trees were affected by acid rain - double the amount affected two years earlier and more than any other country in Europe. Trees affected by acid rain have fewer leaves and their leaves turn yellow.

Most of Britain's air pollution is caused by car exhaust fumes and power stations.

Cycling is often the fastest way to travel around large towns.

Trees take in carbon dioxide from the air to make their own food. At the same time they release oxygen into the air. One large, healthy tree makes enough oxygen for 70 people to breathe.
　　Enough trees to make a forest the size of Wales are cut down every year to provide the paper Britain uses. Most of this paper could be recycled and the trees saved.

Most car journeys in England are less than 3km (2 miles) long.

Some cars have catalytic converters fitted to cut down the poisonous gases in exhaust fumes. When they are working well they absorb up to 80-90% of poisonous fumes. However, they do not work until they have warmed up and they take a long time to heat up. Short journeys cause the most pollution and are the easiest to avoid.

Breathing in the smoke from a cigarette makes more monoxide in your lungs than breathing the air in a street full of traffic.

A jumbo jet can use over 18,000 litres (4,000 gallons) of fuel just to take off. That is about one and a half large fuel tankers.

Cars can only use a quarter of the energy available in petrol. Three-quarters is wasted.

The Shah of Iran said that oil is much too precious to burn and should be made into plastics, medicines and other synthetic things.

British companies spend £5,000,000,000 each year just on packaging their products to make them more attractive. Much of this packaging is unnecessary.

Only a quarter of the world's people live in the rich, industrialised countries of northern America, Europe and Australasia, yet they use four times as much of the Earth's resources - oil, food, metals and so on - as the poorer countries in Africa and Asia. There is not enough for everyone in the world to consume at the rate we do. It is up to us to cut back on what we take from the world by reusing and recycling.

Each year, the average family throws away 4 trees worth of paper, 270 glass bottles and jars, 450 metal cans and 50kg (110lbs) of plastic.

Over half of all plastics that are thrown out could be remoulded and used again. Glass can be melted and reused. Paper and metal can be recycled.

One tonne of recycled glass saves 136 litres (30 gallons) of oil. If all the glass in Britain were recycled, we could save 270 million litres (60,000,000 gallons) of oil each year.

If you turn down the central heating by 1 degree you will be saving 10% of the energy used to heat your home.

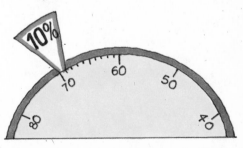

WHAT'S IN A NAME?

If anyone calls you a dunce, you can thank them for paying you a compliment. The word dunce comes from the name of a Scotsman, John Duns Scotus, who was a brilliant scholar in medieval times. He taught philosophy at Oxford, Paris and Cologne and

said that religious beliefs required faith and could not be proved. The Church did not like what Duns Scotus said. Although he was only trying to show that human reason is limited, his theories were distorted after he died. His books were burned and anyone who agreed with Duns Scotus was sneered at and called a Duns!

Lady Godiva.

You may have heard that a woman called Lady Godiva rode through the streets of Coventry naked. Even today such an event would hit the news but in 1040 it was unthinkable. So why did she do it? Lady Godiva was very religious and cared greatly for the people who lived in the region ruled by her husband. Her husband, however, kept

demanding taxes from them. He ignored Lady Godiva's pleas to spare the people, until one day he said he would lift the taxes if she would ride naked through the streets. He was sure she would not do so, but Lady Godiva sent out messengers to ask everyone to close their shutters and not watch. Her long hair covered most of her body as she rode on her horse. Only one person, Peeping Tom, spied on her. Her husband kept his word.

Little Jack Horner.

Jack Horner may have existed. Legend has it that he worked for the Abbot of Glastonbury Abbey in Somerset in the 1530s. The King wanted to abolish the Abbey but the Abbot tried to buy him off. He sent Jack Horner to the King with the deeds of twelve

manor houses on the estate. To keep the deeds safe, the Abbot hid them in a huge pie. It is said that on his way to the King, Jack Horner managed to lift the crust of the pie and pulled out one of the deeds (a plum). Whoever had the deeds owned the manor! It is known that a Thomas Horner did later own one of the manors at Glastonbury.

The Grand Old Duke Of York.

This Duke of York was the second son of George III. In 1793, when he was only 30 years old and still inexperienced, the King put him in charge of the British troops which he sent to Flanders to fight with the Dutch and Austrians against the French. The campaign was not a success, and the rhyme about his marching his troops incompetently up and down the hill became popular. It did not deter the King from appointing the Duke Of York Commander-In-Chief of the whole army in 1798!

Llanfairpwllgwyngyllgogerychwyrn

His next campaign was a failure too. The Duke's main problem was not incompetence, but a badly trained army of ex-convicts and old men. He set up a training school for the officers and improved conditions in the army so that better soldiers could be recruited. But no-one wrote a rhyme about that!

Amelia Bloomer.

Amelia Bloomer argued for women's rights 150 years ago. She wrote books and gave speeches demanding that women be allowed to vote and be educated as well as men. She was also interested in clothes and created her own design. Instead of the tight corsets of the day, she wore loose, baggy trousers under a short skirt. People came to her lectures just to see the strange sight, but stayed to listen to what she had to say. Her bloomers, as they were called, did not catch on until 40 years later, when women started to ride bicycles.

Place names.

The names of towns and villages often go back hundreds of years and refer simply to someone's fort or village. Aber means river mouth, so most towns beginning with it are on the coast. 'Ton' at the end of a name means an estate and the rest of the name may be derived from an ancient owner. Newton is one of the most common place names and simply means new town. 'Ham' and 'by' mean village. 'Chester' means castle. Stranraer in Scotland and Widnes both mean the same thing - broad headland.

Every name has a history. Here are just a few:

Coventry (Cofa's Tree)
Charlton, London (estate of peasants)

Accrington (acorn village)
Aintree, Liverpool (tree that stands on its own)
Arundel (herbal cough medicine)

Banff (suckling pig)
Derby (village with deer)
Elgin (little Ireland)
Ely (eel district)

Glasgow (green hollow)
Goole (sluice or drain)
Harlow (burial mound for the army)
Harrow, London (heathen temple)
Keswick (cheese farm)
Liverpool (sludgy pool)

Leeds (district of people by the violent river)
Swansea (Svenn's island)
Oxford (ford where oxen cross)

The longest place name in Britain is Llanfairpwllgwyngyllgogerychwyrndrobwlllllantysiliogogogoch. It is in Anglesey and is Welsh for 'St. Mary's Church by the pool of the white hazel trees, near the rapid whirlpool, by the red cave of the Church of St. Tysilio'.

At the other extreme, there is a town in Sweden called A and a village in France called Y. There is also a place in Norway called Hell!

FAMOUS PEOPLE

The richest person in Britain is probably the Queen. The total value of her land, house and possessions is estimated to be about £6.5 billion, but most of that does not belong to her personally. It belongs to the crown and cannot be sold. It must be handed down to the next monarch. Her own personal wealth is more likely to be between £150 and £500 million. For the first time ever, the British monarch is about to pay income tax like everyone else. A part of the money she makes each year will be paid to the government.

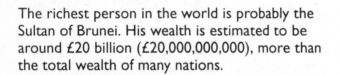

The richest person in the world is probably the Sultan of Brunei. His wealth is estimated to be around £20 billion (£20,000,000,000), more than the total wealth of many nations.

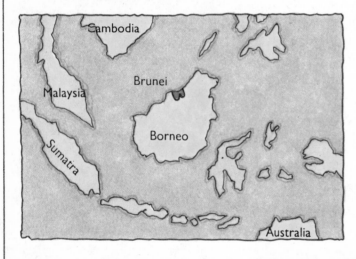

The wealthiest people own many houses and large areas of land. But many people make their wealth in other ways - from sport or entertainment. The tenth richest person in England is Andrew Lloyd Webber who made his fortune from successful musicals, such as *Joseph and the Amazing Technicolour Dreamcoat* and *Cats*.

At least ten people in Britain own more than £240 million of property and possessions. The richest man is Paul Raymond. He owns property valued at £1,400 million.

The Italian opera singer Enrico Caruso left a $9 million fortune when he died in 1922.

Elvis Presley sold more records than anyone else. It is not known exactly how many records he has sold, but he had more than 170 big hits and has sold many million records. It is claimed that if all Elvis's records were stacked on top of one another, the pile would be 80,000 metres (262,480ft) high - nine times as high as Mount Everest.

Elvis was a lorry driver when he first started singing. After his first rock and roll concert, he was advised to stick to lorry driving! Fortunately, he ignored the advice.

The Beatles are the most successful rock group ever. They have sold over 1,000 million records since they recorded 'I Want To Hold Your Hand' in 1963. That song alone has sold 13 million copies worldwide.

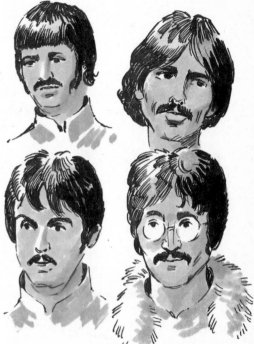

Madonna is the most successful singer today. Her album 'True Blue' has alone sold over 11 million copies around the world. It has a long way to go to rival the most popular song ever - Bing Crosby's 'I'm Dreaming Of A White Christmas', which has sold over 170 million copies. If the song lasts three minutes and all these songs were played one after the other, it would take 969 years to play them all!

Thomas Alva Edison invented records. He called his invention a phonograph and the first song ever recorded was Edison singing 'Mary Had A Little Lamb'.

Enid Blyton has probably written more stories for children than any other children's writer in Britain. She wrote up to 700 different stories, many of which were translated into other languages. The most well known are probably the *Famous Five* series.

The best-selling writer of fiction is Agatha Christie. She wrote 78 crime novels and sold about 2,000 million copies worldwide. Her play *The Mousetrap* is the

longest running play in the world. It opened in London in 1952 and is still running! In that time, the play has been performed over 16,000 times.

The most famous English playwright is William Shakespeare. He wrote 37 plays and no-one knows how often they have been performed since he wrote them about 400 years ago.

ANCIENT WORLD

The Bible tells the story of Noah and the flood. Archaeologists have discovered evidence of a great flood that appeared in Iraq and covered over 1,040 sq km (402 sq miles). The water was so deep, it flooded whole cities and left behind a layer of clay 2.4m (8ft) deep.

In 500 B.C. the Phoenician Hanno was the first European to sail all the way round Africa. When he returned he said that at the southern end of Africa, the sun shone in the north at midday. People laughed at him and said 'impossible', but Hanno was correct and his claim proves that he did indeed reach southern Africa.

When an Egyptian army invaded Syria in 1525 B.C., the soldiers could not believe their eyes - they saw a river falling from the sky and flowing backwards! They had never seen rain before and were so used to the Nile flowing north, that to them, the Euphrates which flowed south, must be flowing backwards.

The people of Mesopotamia had no dustbins. They just used to throw their rubbish onto the streets. It was squashed down by all the people and horses who walked along the street. Nevertheless the houses had to be constantly raised as the level of the streets got higher and higher.

When the Greek historian, Herodotus, visited the pyramids in Egypt more than 2,000 years ago, the pyramids were already 2,000 years old.

Ancient Greek cities, such as Athens, were the first to be governed democratically. Each citizen could go to the senate and take part in government, but not everyone could be a citizen - women, children, foreigners and slaves were all excluded!

In Ancient Greece only boys went to school. Girls learnt to read and write, spin and weave, dance, sing, and keep house, but they learnt at home. Girls of 15 and younger were often married to men twice their age.

Both girls and boys went to school in Ancient Rome, but they had to get up very early for it. School began before dawn and children who were late, or hadn't learnt their lessons, were beaten.

Wealthy Romans did not sit on chairs to eat. They laid on couches around the table and ate with their fingers.

Ancient Rome was a busy and crowded city. So crowded, that tenements five storeys high were built to house the people, and so busy that horses and carts were banned from using the streets by day. Instead they clattered through the city at night and kept everyone awake!

Many of the houses caught fire easily. Only people on the ground floor were allowed to have kitchens, poor people ate cheap food from restaurants instead.

Wealthy Romans had central heating and piped water in their homes. When the Roman Empire collapsed, the technology was forgotten. It was not reinvented until hundreds of years later.

The Roman Empire grew up around the Mediterranean Sea where there are almost no tides. When Julius Caesar invaded Britain in 55 B.C. his soldiers did not pull their boats far enough up the beach. Many of the boats floated away on the high tide.

SPORT

When the Olympic Games was first played in Ancient Greece from 776B.C. until A.D.393 it was very different from today's Olympic Games. The athletes were all naked and no women were allowed to compete or spectate. Athletes did not represent different countries, only themselves. There were no stop watches or record performances, only winners of each event. The events were sprinting, long jump, discus, wrestling and javelin throwing - skills that helped soldiers in the army.

The modern Olympic Games takes place every four years in a different city around the world, and there are over 200 different events. The first time that the ban on women competitors was lifted, was in 1928 when Elizabeth Robinson of the United States competed and won the women's 100m. But it wasn't until 1984, that women were allowed to run in long races such as the 3,000m and the marathon.

Raymond Clarence Ewry of the United States won 10 gold medals between 1900 and 1908 - the most that any competitor has won. The Czechoslovakian gymnast, Vera Caslavska-Odlozil, won 7 gold medals between 1964 and 1968.

In 1954, Roger Bannister made sporting history. He became the first person to run a mile (1609m) in less than four minutes. In 1985, Steve Cram ran a mile in 3 minutes 46.32 seconds. If he had been running with Roger Bannister, Bannister would still have had 88m (96yds) to go when Steve Cram finished.

The American swimmer Mark Spitz won 7 medals at the Munich Games in 1972, the most that any competitor has won in a single Games.

One day in May 1935, the American athlete Jesse Owens broke six world records in less than an hour. He ran the fastest 100 yards, then the fastest 220 yards and 200 metres. He jumped the longest long jump and finally ran the fastest 220 yards and 200 metres hurdles. His record for the long jump of 8.13m (26ft 8in) was not beaten for over 30 years, until 1968.

The following year, Jesse Owens competed in the Olympics in Berlin. At that time Hitler and the Nazis ruled Germany. They believed that fair-haired white people were better then any other people on Earth and Hitler was determined that his chosen athletes would do best in the Games. Jesse Owens quickly disproved this theory when he won several medals!

In 1968, Bob Beamon beat Jesse Owens' long jump record by jumping 8.9m (29ft 2in). This record was unbeaten for 23 years, until Mike Powel jumped 8.95m (29ft 4in) - just a metre less than the length of a double decker bus.

The oldest game.

Dice have been found in the remains of the Assyrian city of Ninevah showing that they were probably played over 3,000 years ago. Chess probably began in Northern India and moved west through Persia to Greece about 2,500 years ago. Draughts is another ancient game. It was played in Egypt over 3,000 years ago.

The most popular sport is fishing. More people fish, than take part in any other sport.

The most successful racing driver is the Argentinian driver, Fangio. In the 1950s he won the World Championship five times, a feat which no other driver has achieved.

The most successful tennis player is the Australian Rod Laver. He won all four major World Championships - the Australian, the French, Wimbledon and the American Open - in the same year. This is called the Grand Slam. Laver is the only player to have won the Grand Slam twice - in 1963 and 1968.

The most successful woman tennis player is the American, Billie Jean King. She won 20 tournaments between 1961 and 1979.

The most successful cricket team is the West Indian team led by Clive Hubert Lloyd from 1974 to 1985. The team won 11 international matches in a row in 1984 and was unbeaten in any match in 1982, 1983 and 1984.

Everyone thinks that the football team they support is the best one, but some teams have a better claim than others. Liverpool has won the League Championship 18 times, and Tottenham Hotspur has won the FA Cup 8 times. Five teams have won both the League Championship and the FA Cup in the same season - Preston North End in 1889, Aston Villa in 1897, Tottenham in 1961, Arsenal in 1971 and Liverpool in 1986.

FACT OR FANTASY?

Ghosts.

Many people claim they have seen ghosts - spirits of people who have died. Some phantoms have even been photographed. But no-one has been able to prove that these apparitions are the spirits of dead people. What happens after death is a mystery, and whether you believe in an afterlife is a matter of faith. Some ghosts may be a trick of the light or a hallucination. A hallucination is when you think you see something that is not there.

Poltergeists.

These restless spirits are supposed to throw things around the room. Some have been reported to be quite violent and dangerous. But even in Britain there are many minor earthquakes which we scarcely feel, but which may shake a building enough to cause things to fall off shelves.

Telepathy.

Can people read other people's minds? And do some people have a sixth sense which enables them to predict the future? There are many examples of people changing their travel arrangements at the last minute and so escaping a plane or train crash. Identical twins often claim to know what the other is thinking and even to know when they are in pain.

Scientific investigation.

The supernatural seems to hate scientific laboratories. Experiments have been set up with clairvoyants - people who can see things that are going on out of their range of vision. Clairvoyants have been asked to guess what shapes are on hidden cards, but the number of correct answers are not significantly better than those chosen by chance. But, say the clairvoyants, predicting shapes on a card has no emotional importance - unlike an impending disaster. The police have used clairvoyants to help them solve murders and look for missing people.

The difficulty of investigating supernatural phenomena using scientific equipment is illustrated by toci-toci beetles. The male beetle attracts a mate by tapping on a stone. He can be heard by females up to 5km (3 miles) away, but no sound can be detected by

even the most sensitive microphones. Those who believe in the supernatural, might say that just because the microphone does not pick up the sound, it does not prove that something is not happening. The scientists might say that the females do not use supernatural powers to detect the male, but hear the sound waves caused by his tapping.

Nostradamus lived in France over 400 years ago. He wrote at great length and, it is claimed, predicted many things that subsequently happened, such as the Fire Of London in 1666 and the rise of General Franco in Spain in the 1930s. He even predicted his own death.

However, when you look closely at the writings of Nostradamus they are so vague and confused you could read almost any reading you like into them. Perhaps time will tell. He is said to have predicted that the next Pope will be the last.

Whether you believe in the supernatural very much depends on whether you want to believe in it. About 4,000 years ago people in ancient China believed that when the sun set in the

evening, it was eaten by a dragon. Every evening the people beat their drums loudly to scare away the dragon and it worked. Next morning the sun rose again!

Uri Geller is well known for being able to bend metal by simply stroking it. But does he have supernatural powers? Many magicians and conjurers can produce the same effect by trickery.

The word 'lunatic' comes from the Latin word for moon. Are people more mad when the moon is full? Investigations do not show it, but they do show there is more crime around full moon.

Several years ago people in Britain were puzzled by strange circles and shapes that appeared overnight in fields of corn. Were they made by beings from another planet? Some people argued that no human could have made such perfect circles without leaving tracks in the rest of the corn. The argument raged for several months, before the people causing the shapes admitted to their tricks.

There is an area in the Caribbean Sea known as the Bermuda Triangle. Many ships and planes have mysteriously disappeared here. Is there some supernatural force at work here, spiriting people away to another planet or pulling them to their death in the sea below? Although many

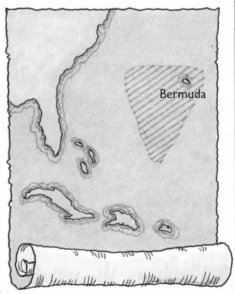

Bermuda

disappearances are reported to have happened in calm weather, investigations show that the area is given to sudden storms. Hurricanes often begin here and it is not surprising that many planes and ships have been lost.

Atlantis.

The Ancient Greeks write of an idyllic island called Atlantis which disappeared into the sea. Why did it disappear? According to the story, the sea god was so angry at how greedy and dishonest the people had become, he shook the island for a day and a night

before the sea swamped it forever. Many people have wondered whether Atlantis really existed and historians think that the legend is based on the island of Thera, now known as Santorini. In 1450B.C. a huge volcanic explosion shook the island. Most of the island disappeared beneath the sea and a tidal wave flooded the island round about, probably destroying the Minoan civilisation of the nearby island, Crete.

Who sold the first hamburgers?

The brothers, Maurice and Richard MacDonald set up business near Pasadena in 1940.

What is your Achilles' Heel?

Your weak spot! The Greek hero Achilles was dipped in the River Styx by his mother. This protected him from harm - except the heel by which she held him. One day he was killed by an arrow in his heel!

Does the colour red make a bull angry?

The bull is colour blind and does not see red at all. It charges the bullfighter's cape because it is waved in front of it, and this makes the bull mad!

What is a jumping bean?

Have you seen a Mexican bean jump? A tiny caterpillar, living inside the bean, moves around when it is warm. It changes into a moth and emerges from the bean through the hole it made as a caterpillar.

What is smoke?

The gases and unburned fuel that rise with the hot air from a fire. Smoke contains acids that harm plant life and corrode buildings.

Who played the pipes of Pan?

Pan was the Greek God of flocks and herds. He was half man and half goat and he had pointed ears, goat's horns and hooves. He played on a set of panpipes.

Who made the Tin Lizzie?

In 1908 Henry Ford, the American car manufacturer made a car for everybody. He made 15 million cars by mass production.

Why do men raise their hats?

In the Middle Ages knights would raise their visors to show they were friends not foes, and the tradition has continued as a gesture of politeness.

Is the Earth round?

It is almost spherical in shape. It bulges out a little at the equator and is slightly flatter at the poles.

Was Cleopatra an Egyptian?

The Queen of Egypt was of Greek descent. She was almost certainly born in the city of Alexandria, which was a major Greek city in those days.

Why was the Panama Canal built?

It enabled ships to take a short cut between the Atlantic and the Pacific, and avoid going around Cape Horn. The first ship passed through the 82km (51mile) long canal in 1914.

Who named New York?

At first the Dutch named it New Amsterdam. In 1664 the British took over the settlement and re-named it New York after the Duke of York, brother of Charles!

Who was Echo?

In Greek mythology the nymph Echo fell in love with Narcissus. Because he didn't return her love, she faded into just an answering voice.

What happened to Narcissus?

As a punishment, he fell in love with his own reflection. Like Echo, he pined away and was changed into the flower named Narcissus.

Who found the Victoria Falls?

David Livingstone the Scottish missionary and explorer. He traced the course of the Zambesi in Africa and discovered Lake Malawi and the Victoria Falls.

What flavour comes from an orchid?

The scented seed pods from certain kinds of orchid flavour sweet dishes and drinks with vanilla. The Aztecs used to flavour chocolate drinks with the pods.

Is the Pekinese from China?

The Chinese have bred these dogs for over 5,000 years. Only members of their royal family were allowed to own them. Five of these dogs were brought secretly to Europe in 1898.

Can you find the Moon in a window?

In 1969 rock from the Moon was brought back to Earth by Apollo astronauts. A tiny piece is sealed in a stained glass window in Washington Cathedral, USA.

Who built the Ark?

Noah was warned by God of a great flood. He built an ark big enough to take his family and two of every species of animal. When the flood was over the ark came to rest on Mount Ararat.

How old is Mickey Mouse?

This world famous mouse was first seen in the cartoon *Steam Boat Willie* in 1928. His creator Walt Disney used his own voice for the mouse.

Are elephants afraid of mice?

This is completely false. Mice are often found in elephants' cages in zoos and circuses. The two animals don't seem to notice each other at all.

How does an octopus move?

To propel itself through the water, it squirts water backwards from a tube under its head.

What is the Milky Way?

It is a galaxy of millions of stars that stretch in a milky white band across the sky at night.

Where are the Antipodes?

Places exactly opposite each other through the centre of the globe. To people living in Britain, the Antipodes are Australia and New Zealand.

What is liquorice?

It is made from the roots of the liquorice plant which is crushed and the juice extracted. When it solidifies, it is made into glossy black sticks to be used in sweets, drinks and medicines.

Who sings the Marseillaise?

It is the French national anthem composed in 1792. It was first sung in Paris at the time of the French Revolution.

When did the first crossword appear?

On December 21 1913 in the *New York World*. It was compiled by American journalist Arthur Wynne.

What was Eskimo-pie?

The name of the first choc-ice! It was invented by an American called C.K. Nelson in 1922 and given the name Eskimo-pie.

What was the guillotine?

A machine for cutting off the heads of all the people sentenced to death. Named after Dr Guillotin who suggested its use.

How much do you drink in your lifetime?

The average person drinks 50,000 litres (11,000 gallons) of liquid.

Does a pencil contain lead?

The lead in pencils is made from graphite which is a form of carbon found in layers between rock.

What is on Easter Island?

On a small isolated island in the south eastern Pacific are scattered about 1,000 giant statues. Some weigh up to 90 tonnes and are 9.5m (32ft) tall. No one really knows how the Polynesians carved or raised these statues.

What large animal was first discovered in 1900?

The okapi is a shy animal related to the giraffe. It lives in the dense rainforests of central Africa and eats a diet of leaves and shoots. It was completely unknown until 1900.

Is an iceberg salty?

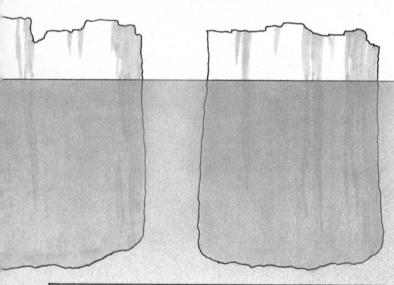

Found in the Arctic and Antarctic regions, icebergs are floating masses of ice that have broken away from a glacier. They float in the sea, carried by currents in the water and the wind. Gradually they are melted by the sun and the warm water into which they drift. They are not salty because they are made of snow!

Do bananas grow on trees?

They grow on tropical plants as tall as trees, up to 3m (10ft) high. The bananas grow on a single stalk, often 70-160 fruit in one bunch. The plant is cut down but grows back again next season.

Where do you find gargoyles?

Stonemasons in the Middle Ages carved animal heads, devils and grotesque faces as water spouts. They took rainwater from church or cathedral roofs and kept the water clear of the stone walls.

What is a mummy?

A dead body that has been embalmed or preserved and sometimes wrapped in hundreds of metres of bandages. The name mummy comes from the Persian word 'mummia', which means 'tar'. Because the bodies were black with age, people wrongly believed they had been soaked in tar.

Who was Hannibal and how did he cross the Alps?

He was the leader of the Carthaginian army who invaded Italy in 218 BC. He took an army of 40,000 men and 37 elephants over the Pyrenees and the Alps from Spain to Italy. Hannibal floated his elephants across rivers on huge rafts - but he never conquered Rome!

What is perspective?

To draw solid objects you give the impression of distance or depth by making parallel lines converge to a vanishing point at eye level or on the horizon.

What are stalactites and stalagmites?

Stalactites are formed in limestone caves by the constant dripping of water from the roof. Limestone deposits cause shapes like icicles to form from the ceiling of caves. Water drips from them onto the floor and a stalagmite is produced. After thousands of years the two may grow together to make a solid pillar.

Is a sponge a plant or an animal?

A sponge is one of the simplest forms of animal life. It feeds by drawing in water through its pores and extracting food. We use the dead skeleton of a sponge to wash with in the bath!

Where does a female puffin lay her eggs?

Although puffins spend most of their time far out at sea, they also rest on rocks and cliffs in large colonies.

These birds dig long burrows in the ground using their beaks and feet. Their eggs are laid in a little nesting chamber at the end of the underground burrow.

Who lives at Number Ten?

The official residence of British Prime Ministers is number 10 Downing Street. It is in a side-street off Whitehall, near the Houses of Parliament.

It was built by Sir George Downing in 1680, and in 1738 George II offered it to Sir Robert Walpole, who was Britain's first Prime Minister.

Next door, at number 11, lives the Chancellor of the Exchequer.

How can you draw an ellipse?

To draw a perfect oval or ellipse, stick two pins through a paper covered board. Join them with a thread that is longer than the distance between the pins. Put a pencil in the thread, keep it tight and draw an ellipse.

What is a Möbius strip?

To make a Möbius strip, take a strip of paper, give it half a twist, then join the ends to form a band. Run a pencil round and you'll find the strip has one single edge. It was named after the 19th century mathematician Augustus Möbius.

Who lives at the White House?

It is the official residence of the President of the United States of America. It is in Washington, the capital.

The White House was designed by an Irish architect and the foundation stone was laid in 1792. President John Adams was its first occupant in 1880.

The house was originally built of grey Virginian sandstone, but in August 1814 it was burned by British troops. After the war it was painted white to hide the marks made by the smoke.

Why do flowers smell?

To humans some flowers smell sweet and others smell disgusting. Certain flowers, that have an odour of decay are pollinated by flies and sometimes bats.

Some insects visit scented flowers to feed on pollen and sweet smelling nectar. As insects go from flower to flower they spread pollen, which in turn helps to make the seeds for next season's plants.

Who found the Dead Sea Scrolls?

One day in 1947, a Bedouin boy was looking for a lost goat along the cliffs by the Dead Sea. He threw a stone into the mouth of some caves and heard the sound of breaking pottery.

Once inside he discovered several clay jars containing decayed parchment scrolls, on which were written Bible stories over 2,000 years old. These and many other manuscripts found in caves nearby, became known as the Dead Sea Scrolls - one of the most important discoveries of all time!

Who was Johnny Appleseed?

His real name was John Chapman. All his life he roamed Ohio Territory planting apple seeds and trees. He walked barefoot, even in winter. His clothes were ragged, he wore an upturned pot on his head and carried a Bible in his shirt.

What is the most poisonous creature in the sea?

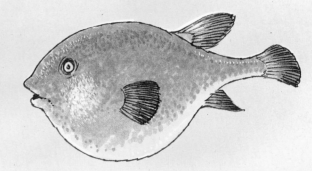

The puffer fish, which puffs itself up when threatened, is one of the world's most poisonous fish. They are eaten in Japan, after careful preparation by a trained chef, who removes the poisonous sac.

This delicacy is known as a fugu and is eaten raw. Many people die each year from eating this dish. The poison paralyses the nervous system and there is no known antidote.

Which famous storyteller was a cobbler's son?

Hans Christian Andersen was born in Odense, Denmark. He was the son of a poor sick cobbler, who died when Hans was eleven.

At the age of fourteen he went to Copenhagen to become an actor or singer, but everyone laughed at him. For a time he walked the streets, hungry, lonely and friendless.

In the years to come he tried all kinds of writing, but without success. At last a play of his was performed at the Royal Theatre, and when his first book of fairy tales was published four years later, he became famous overnight.

He will always be remembered for such well known stories as *The Ugly Duckling*, *The Snow Queen*, *The Emperor's New Clothes*, *The Tinderbox* and many more.

Where is the statue of the Little Mermaid?

Sitting on a rock in Copenhagen harbour is a bronze statue of the Little Mermaid. She is the heroine of one of Hans Christian Andersen's best known fairy tales.

Who were the brothers Grimm?

The brothers Jacob and Wilhelm, two language professors, collected old folk tales told in Germany. They published them as a collection of fairy tales. *Snow White*, *Hansel and Gretel*, *Rumpelstiltskin* and *Rapunzel* were just a few.

Who wrote *Cinderella*?

Red Riding Hood, *Puss in Boots*, *Sleeping Beauty* and *Cinderella* were all written in France by Charles Perrault in the 18th century.

Who was Scheherazade?

The stories in the *Arabian Nights* were told by Scheherazade to her husband the King. He always killed his wives the day after they were married.

Scheherazade did not die, because every night she told him a different story and stopped at the most exciting part. Each morning the King spared her life and waited to hear that night how the story ended.

Some of the stories she told were *The Seven Voyages of Sinbad* and *Aladdin*.

Who translated these stories into English?

Sir Richard Burton the Victorian explorer, who together with Captain John Speke, led expeditions across East Africa to discover the source of the River Nile. As an old man he translated the *Arabian Nights*.

Who was Lewis Carroll?

His real name was Charles Lutwidge Dodgson, and he was a lecturer in mathematics at Oxford. Lewis Carroll was better known as the author of *Alice in Wonderland*. The story was told to his friends' children - one of whom was a nine-year-old girl called Alice.

Who was the boy who wouldn't grow up?

On December 27th 1904, a new play for children opened in London. It was J.M. Barrie's *Peter Pan*, the boy from Never Never Land who wouldn't grow up, together with Wendy, the Lost Boys and the evil Captain Hook. It became the most famous play ever written for children.

How did Mark Twain get his name?

The American writer's real name was Samuel L. Clemens. For a time he worked on a Mississippi steamboat as a river pilot. The boatmen shouted 'mark twain' (second mark) as they measured the shallow water to a depth of two fathoms (3.6m or 12 ft).

Best known of his humorous books are *The Adventures of Tom Sawyer* and *The Adventures of Huckleberry Finn*.

Which writer was the Secretary of the Bank of England?

Kenneth Graham who wrote *The Wind in the Willows* was a banker. His stories of Mole, Rat, Toad and Badger were first published in 1908.

Who wrote the *Just So* stories?

Rudyard Kipling was born in India and wrote many stories about the animals and people there. His *Jungle Book* tells of an Indian boy Mowgli, who was brought up with wolves. In the tale he becomes friendly with the animals and helps them overcome their enemies. In the *Just So* stories, Kipling tells how the leopard got its spots, the elephant its trunk, and the camel its hump!

Was Sherlock Holmes a real detective?

No, he was not a real person, but he was probably the most famous fictional detective of all time!

In 60 stories written by Edinburgh doctor Sir Arthur Conan Doyle, Sherlock Holmes and his friend Dr Watson lived in London at 221B Baker Street. Amazing powers of observation and deduction helped Holmes solve the most bizarre of crimes.

When did we domesticate animals?

The earliest animals to live together with humans were goats, sheep, cattle, pigs and dogs.

Stone Age people had wolf-like dogs around their camps over 10,000 years ago, and may have hunted with them. Goats and sheep were first domesticated in the Middle East, and provided early human beings with milk, wool and skins around 8,000BC.

Rabbits first lived with us as recently as AD1,000.

What are hieroglyphics?

They are a system of picture writing used by the ancient Egyptian priests. At first, pictorial symbols represented words that were easily recognised like man, bird, flower, Sun and eye. Later, as hieroglyphics developed, some symbols were used to represent sounds.

Modern scholars could not understand this writing until the early 1800s.

How was the mystery of hieroglyphics solved?

The puzzle of this strange writing was solved in 1799 when a large black stone was discovered near Rosetta in Egypt.

It told the same story repeated in hieroglyphics, ancient Greek and demotic. It was finally deciphered in 1822 by Jean Champollion when the riddle of the Rosetta Stone was solved.

What was Archimedes' great discovery in the bath?

Archimedes was a great mathematician and scientist born in 287 BC. He is mostly remembered for discovering a fact that became known as 'Archimedes' Principle'. All bodies weighed when immersed in fluid, show a loss of weight equal to the fluid they displace.

Archimedes made this startling discovery while he was in his bath. He was so excited that he rushed out in the street naked shouting "Eureka!" This is Greek for "I have found it!"

Who planted the first apple trees in Australia?

The ship The Bounty was commanded by Captain Bligh. In 1787 some of the crew, led by Fletcher Christian, mutinied against Bligh's cruel discipline and set him and 18 sailors adrift in a small boat.

This tiny boat crossed 5,793km (3,600 miles) of open sea and landed safely in the East Indies.

In 1805 Bligh was made governor of New South Wales and he planted Australia's first apple trees.

How long would it take to boil an ostrich egg?

To soft boil a hen's egg for breakfast would take four minutes. An ostrich's egg, the biggest bird's egg of all, would take at least 40 minutes to boil.

Where does chocolate come from?

The main ingredient of chocolate is cocoa from the fruit of the cacao tree. The fruit is the size of a small melon and contains around 40 beans that are dried, roasted, then ground into a fine powder.

The Aztecs drank an unsweetened chocolate drink, often mixed with wine and flavoured with pimento and pepper.

In the mid-nineteenth century solid chocolate bars were made in Europe from cocoa powder, cocoa butter, sugar and sometimes milk.

What happened to the American buffalo?

The American buffalo is really a bison. Millions of them roamed across the plains of North America before the arrival of white people.

The Indians hunted them for food, clothes, tepees - even some of their boats were covered in buffalo hide - but their numbers remained the same.

During the 1800s they were hunted almost to extinction, to help feed the thousands of men employed in building the new railroads and for their cheap hides. In 1889 their numbers had dropped from 20,000,000 to just over 1,000. Luckily the remaining herds are now protected.

What is a monolith?

Ayers Rock in the desert plains of central Australia is one of the world's largest monoliths, which means an upright single stone. It is 348m (1,143ft) high and nearly 9km (6 miles) round.

This eroded sandstone mountain is a sacred place to the Australian Aborigines - in the large caves at the base of the rock, the walls are decorated with their early paintings.

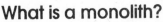

Is the koala a bear?

Although koalas look like small bears, they are related to the ring-tailed possum and the great glider, and are not bears at all!

They spend between 18 and 20 hours a day resting, and four to six hours munching the leaves of eucalyptus trees.

What is a laughing jackass?

A type of kingfisher called the kookaburra has a call that sounds like loud, hysterical laughter. These birds live in the grasslands of Australia, often near water. They hunt snakes, mice and insects.

Why do camels have big feet?

Camels are specially adapted for travelling across the desert. They do not sink into the sand because their feet have broad soles that cover a large area, so the pressure on the sand is low.

Who first brought tobacco to England?

Sir Walter Raleigh introduced pipe-smoking into court circles in 1586. He was a great favourite with Queen Elizabeth I. Unfortunately, after her death he fell out of favour. He was imprisoned for 12 years and then beheaded.

Why are the eggs of some birds pointed?

A pointed egg will roll round in a circle! The eggs of certain sea birds are this shape so they do not roll off the cliff edges where the birds breed.

Why does a peacock display his feathers?

The peacock is the male bird, the female peahen has plain brown feathers and a small tail. The peacock spreads his brilliant fan-like tail to attract the female.

What is an angler fish?

This saltwater fish has a thin spine that grows from its head - just like a fishing rod! On the end is a growth that looks like a piece of bait. This attracts smaller fish, which the angler quickly gobbles up.

Who really invented the telephone?

Alexander Graham Bell and Elisha Gray both filed applications for the patent on the very same day in New York, January 14 1876. Bell arrived at the Patent Office at 12.00 noon, Gray at 2.00pm.

After a long court case, judges decided that Bell invented the telephone.

How can you tell the age of a tree?

Each year as the tree grows it adds a new ring of sap wood beneath the bark. If the tree is cut down, you can estimate its age by counting the rings on a cross-section of the trunk.

Which was the last planet to be discovered?

The ninth planet, Pluto, was discovered by a young American astronomer, Clyde Tombaugh, in 1930. Pluto is 5,970 million km (3,700 million miles) from the Sun and has one moon.

What was a quagga?

A type of wild horse with stripes like a zebra. Vast herds once roamed the plains of South Africa. It was hunted for its skin and became extinct. The last quagga was seen in 1875.

Why do sailors sleep in hammocks?

Until the hammock was invented, sailors simply slept on the wooden decks.

On one of his voyages to the West Indies, Sir John Hawkins came across some of the natives sleeping in hanging beds slung from two trees. They called them 'hammacoes'. So, from 1586 on, all sailors on Sir John's ships slept in hammocks - and the habit spread to seafarers all over the world.

Who fought in a tournament?

In the Middle Ages, knights on horseback fought one another in mock battles or tournaments for sport and entertainment.

Jousting took place in the tilting-yard in a special enclosure surrounded by stands for spectators. Two knights in full armour would charge at each other on either side of a wooden barrier, each one trying to unseat the other. Although they carried blunt lances, injuries were common.

The tournaments were really a chance for knights to practise ready for real battles or war.

Who was King Canute?

He was the son of the King of Denmark and he ruled England from 1016-1035.

When his courtiers became too flattering, saying he was all powerful and could do anything, King Canute decided to prove them wrong!

He had his throne placed on the beach in front of the incoming tide. As the water lapped around his feet, he ordered the waves to stop and the tide to go back. Of course it did not! This way the wise King showed he had the powers of a man and not a god.

Where is Table Mountain?

Cape Town, South Africa, lies at the foot of Table Mountain. This majestic flat-topped mountain sometimes has a flat white cloud covering the top, that looks just like a tablecloth!

What is the Pentagon?

A huge five-sided building in Alexandria, Virginia, across the Potomac River from Washington DC. It houses the US Defence Department's offices for the army, navy, air force and coastguard.

You could fit eighty-three soccer pitches into the 604,000 sq. m (6,500,000 sq. ft) floor area, and spend all day running up and down the 28 km (17.5 miles) of corridors.

Who has been surfing for centuries?

Although the sport of surfing reached California around 1900, it was seen much earlier by Captain Cook in 1778, when he arrived in Hawaii.

The sport probably came to Hawaii when the Tahitians migrated there over 1,000 years earlier.

Which is the red planet?

In the reflected light of the Sun, the planet Mars shines red. The surface is made up of dry plains, mountains and craters. The redness is caused by the dust and oxidation of the rocks.

Who made the first sandwich?

John Montagu, the fourth Earl of Sandwich, is said to have invented the sandwich in 1762.

The Earl loved to gamble, and so as not to interrupt his card game a servant was ordered to bring him a piece of meat between two slices of buttered bread. That is how the Earl gave his name to the sandwich!

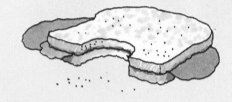

Which famous dog was rescued from a battle-field?

During the First World War, a tiny puppy trembling with shock was rescued from a German trench by an American soldier, Captain Lee Duncan.

The soldier took the puppy back to America, trained him and taught him tricks. The dog was called Rin Tin Tin, the German shepherd who became the most popular animal film star in the world!

What was a crinoline?

A hooped petticoat that was fashionable in the middle of the 19th century. The billowing skirts of Victorian times were held in place by a steel or whale-boned frame called a crinoline, which hung from the waist. It made the wearer's skirt look like a huge bell.

Underneath their crinolines, women wore several lacy petticoats and a pair of long pantaloons - just in case a strong wind blew!

Crinolines became so wide that women wearing them could not squeeze through a door or walk down the stairs - even sitting on a chair was difficult!

Was Julius Caesar a Roman Emperor?

Julius Caesar (102-44BC) was a Roman statesman and a general who conquered Gaul (now France and Belgium), and invaded Britain in 55BC.

He became the sole ruler and dictator of the Roman Empire, but was never the emperor.

He was stabbed to death in the Senate House by enemies who believed that he had too much power.

Who was Aesop?

He is thought to have been a slave who lived in Asia Minor in the 6th century BC.

He is remembered for the stories that he wrote and collected.

Which birds have the most beautiful feathers?

Birds of paradise from northern Australia and New Guinea are among the most colourful birds in the world.

To attract a mate, some birds show off their amazing plumage by hanging upside-down like an acrobat and spreading their tail feathers out.

Who hunts them?

The tribesmen of New Guinea make head-dresses from the beautiful feathers of these birds. They even wear the long tail feathers through their noses.

What were his stories called?

His stories were called fables; short tales with a moral. Aesop's fables had animal characters such as the tortoise and the hare:

A hare once challenged a tortoise to a race. The hare knew he was quicker than the tortoise so he rested on the way. The slow tortoise took his time, but he won the race. The hare was so confident that he had fallen asleep!

Where would you find a tuatara?

The tuatara is a reptile found only in parts of New Zealand. It belongs to the stegosaurus family and has remained unchanged for over 200 million years. It is our only living contact with the dinosaurs.

The stegosaurus hunts at night, but don't worry - it's only about 75cm (30in) long!

What is cork?

It is the outer bark of the cork oak tree, which grows in large numbers in Spain and Portugal. When a tree is 20-years-old the bark is cut and peeled off in rectangular pieces. This is repeated every 10 years, but it does not harm the tree. Cork is very light and floats on water.

Is the umbrella a modern invention?

The pharaoahs of ancient Egypt sat under ceremonial 'brollies' held by slaves. The Chinese used them before 1,000BC, but only royalty or court officials. Some looked like pagodas, four umbrellas high. King Louis XIII of France owned the first waterproof umbrella in 1637.

At the battle of Waterloo, English officers on

horseback held an umbrella in one hand and a sabre in the other. The Duke of Wellington's umbrella was made of oiled cotton with a concealed sword inside!

What did the Duke of Wellington give his name to?

During his campaigns in Belgium and Spain, the first Duke of Wellington got his feet muddy so he had a special pair of waterproof boots designed that reached as far as the knee - Wellingtons!

What happened to Pompeii?

Pompeii was a fashionable Roman town in the bay of Naples at the foot of Mount Vesuvius. On the morning of August 24th in the year AD79, there was a great crash, the ground shook and the sky went dark. The volcano Vesuvius had erupted so violently and suddenly that within a few hours the town of Pompeii was buried under layers of pumice and volcanic ash which rained down from above.

Many people were able to run from the city, but about 2,000 died, covered with a blanket of ash about three metres (10ft) deep. Four other nearby towns disappeared in the eruption including Herculaneum.

For hundreds of years the towns were forgotten, until in 1710 a peasant digging deep for a well found pieces of marble that were from Herculaneum.

Then in 1748 the town of Pompeii was discovered, but the main excavations did not begin on a large scale until 1860.

Digging revealed rows of shops, hundreds of homes, theatres, public baths and a huge amphitheatre. Even the food that had been left ready on the tables for lunch that day in AD 79 (bread, fruit, walnuts, sausages and eggs) had been preserved by the volcanic ash. Plaster casts have been made of the people and animals that lived and died there.

You can visit the ruins of Pompeii today and see what life was really like in Roman times, almost two thousand years ago.

What is pumice stone?

A very light and porous rock that floats in water. Pumice stone is found in volcanic areas.

It is formed by the quick cooling of molten volcanic lava as it pours out of the volcano. Air bubbles are trapped inside the rock from the foaming white hot lava. When the stone solidifies, gases inside are released and form tiny air pockets making the pumice stone feel very light.

Which is the world's smallest independent state?

It is the Vatican City in Italy, which has been the residence of the popes since the fifth century AD. It has a population of around 1,000, and no one is ever born there! The Vatican is the government centre of the Roman Catholic Church.

It lies within the boundaries of Rome, and covers an area of just 0.44 sq. m (0.17 sq. miles).

This tiny state has its own guards, money, flag, post-office, railway station, bank and daily newspaper. It also has a broadcasting station and telephone system. There's even an astronomical observatory!

Early in the 16th century, Pope Julius II asked Michaelangelo to design a uniform for the papal guard in the Vatican City. At the time there were 6,000 men in this army, all recruited from Switzerland. Nowadays there are only about 100 Swiss guards, but their uniform is exactly the same as that designed by Michaelangelo in the 1500s.

Millions of people visit the Vatican every year. Most of them come to see the Basilica of St Peters with its magnificent frescoes of biblical scenes painted on the ceiling of the Sistine Chapel.

What are frescoes?

They are paintings done in watercolour on walls or ceilings while the plaster is still wet. The painting must be finished before the plaster dries. The colours sink into the plaster and remain fresh and bright, often for hundreds of years.

Who was Michaelangelo?

He was an Italian painter, sculptor and architect who designed the great dome of St Peters. He is best known for his sculpture and his paintings in the Sistine Chapel. To reach the ceiling, Michaelangelo had to work on a scaffold lying flat on his back, often working long hours by candlelight.

The whole masterpiece took four years. During that time Michaelangelo painted 340 figures and covered 10,000 square feet of ceiling!

Who was Mother Goose?

No one knows who Mother Goose was, but her tales and rhymes have been told for centuries.

In 1696 some were written down by a French man Charles Perrault. Then they were published in Paris as a book containing eight stories.

Mother Goose tales were first translated into English in 1729. Then in 1785 some of our best loved nursery rhymes appeared in books in America.

What was a penny farthing?

This early bicycle got its name from the wheels, which resembled two English coins of the time, the large penny and the small farthing.

It was invented in 1871 in Coventry, England, by James Starley. For every turn of the pedals, a gear turned the big front wheel twice!

Did Lord Nelson ever suffer from sea sickness?

Lord Horatio Nelson, the most famous of all English admirals, joined the navy at the age of 12, but suffered from sea sickness all his life. He was killed during the Battle of Trafalgar in 1805.

Why does the Tower of Pisa lean?

Pisa is a town in northern Italy famous for its leaning tower, a campanile (bell tower) built for the cathedral and designed to carry the sound of bells as far as possible.

The white marble tower is 54.5m (179ft) high and weighs 14,150 tonnes. It leans because the foundations are not strong enough, just 3m (10ft) deep.

The building was started in 1173 and began to lean almost immediately. It took 200 years to complete, and the tower has tilted more over the years. The top is now 5.6m (18ft) out of true.

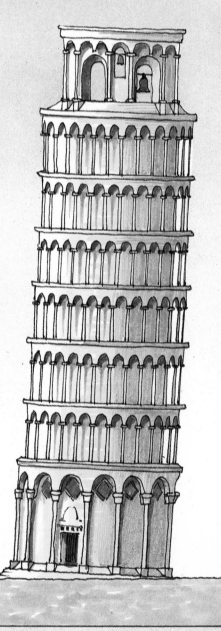

Who were the first people to climb Mount Everest?

The highest mountain in the world above sea level is Mount Everest in the Himalayas. It is 8,849m (29,030ft) high, although the depth of ice on the peak changes this a little.

It was first climbed in 1953 by Sir Edmund Hillary and the Sherpa, Tensing Norgay. They planted the flags of Britain, Nepal, India and the U.N. on the top.

Was Robinson Crusoe a real person?

Daniel Defoe's novel *Robinson Crusoe*, published in 1719, was based on the true story of a Scottish sailor Alexander Selkirk. After a quarrel at sea, he was left, at his own request, on the island of Juan Fernandez, Chile. He was rescued four years later.

Do ostriches really bury their heads in the sand?

No, when danger threatens, an ostrich may run away, often at 80.5km (50 miles) an hour. But it can also inflict terrible wounds by kicking out with its powerful legs and sharp toes.

What was the wooden horse of Troy?

This story is told in Homer's poem, the *Iliad*. Troy in Asia Minor, had been under siege by the Greeks for 10 years. The Greeks tricked the Trojans into opening the city gates for a great wooden horse, which was full of soldiers hidden inside. Once the gates were opened the Greek army followed and captured Troy.

What is a tornado?

A violent and destructive column of spinning air. A whirlwind with a wind speed at its centre that can reach 640kmh (400mph). This swirling funnel shaped cloud travels forward at about 65kmh (40mph) causing terrible destruction.

Do you know what cotton is?

Cotton grows on low bushes in the south eastern states of the USA, Egypt, Brazil and India. It is the fluffy tufts of white fibre (bolls) that grow round the cotton seeds.
Cotton is picked, and after cleaning it is spun into thread that can be woven into cloth.

How do you charm a snake?

Snakes cannot hear the music played to them by a snake charmer because they are deaf!
They copy the movements of the snake charmer and his flute - swinging from side to side as if they are hypnotised.

What did Laslo Biro invent?

In 1938 he invented the ballpoint pen. He was a Hungarian journalist and realised that the quick-drying ink he had seen used by the printing trade could be adapted for use in a pen.

What is a flying boat?

It is an aircraft that can land and take off from water. The underside of the plane is shaped like a boat. Each wing has a float underneath to keep the plane balanced in the water. Some, called amphibians, have wheels and can be used on land or on water.

What is different about the mule?

It is a hybrid animal with a donkey for a father and a horse for a mother. It has the strength of a horse, and is as hardy and as sure-footed as a donkey.

They are mainly used as pack animals, especially on rough roads. Mules can be quite stubborn at times!

Why is the sky blue?

The sky has no colour of its own. When sunlight (made up of all colours) passes through the atmosphere it is scattered around by millions of particles in the air.

The blue in the sunlight is scattered more than the other colours, so the sky appears to be blue.

Did cavemen ever hunt dinosaurs?

Dinosaurs have been extinct for more than 60 million years. Humans appeared on Earth two to four million years ago. The two have only met in stories and cartoons, or in films and television.

Do whales spout water?

Whales are mammals and must return to the surface of the water to breathe air. The whale's spout is its exhaled breath from a hole on the top of its head.

Whales are really spouting air, not water at all!

Where does sand come from?

Sand is made up of lots of bits of mineral substances, mostly silica or quartz. It is formed by the breaking down and weathering of rocks.

On the seashore, sand often contains minute particles of shell.

Did you know there are plants that eat insects?

The Venus flytrap closes, traps, then digests any insect that lands on its hair-covered leaves.

The pitcher plant captures insects that venture over the rim then fall to the bottom. A few plants grow large enough to trap small reptiles and animals. Some pitcher plants can open their lids and let rainwater in to drown their prey.

Venus flytrap

Pitcher plants

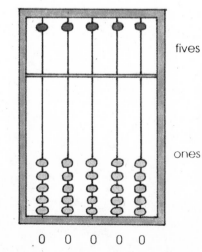

What is the world's largest and smelliest flower?

The rafflesia plant is the largest and smelliest! Up to 90cm (3ft) across, and weighing 7kg (15lb).

What is an abacus?

It is an ancient calculating machine, dating 5,000 years, that is still in use today.

Rows of beads threaded on wire represent units, tens, hundreds etc. To calculate, the beads are moved up and down or sideways.

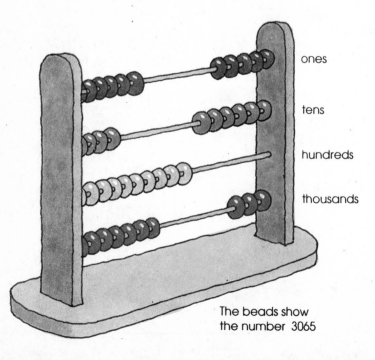

ones

tens

hundreds

thousands

The beads show the number 3065

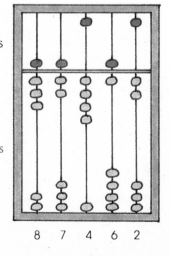

fives

ones

0 0 0 0 0   8 7 4 6 2

Did you know there are two types of camel?

The Bactrian camel from central Asia has two humps. The Arabian camel bred in S.E. Asia has one. The Arabian is taller and faster, and when bred for racing is known as a dromedary. The Bactrian is much sturdier and can carry heavy loads.

Do they store water in their humps?

A camel can extract some water from the food reserve of fat in the hump. It does not need to sweat to keep cool until its body temperature reaches 46°C (115°F).

Arabian Camel   Bactrian Camel

What is an optical illusion?

It occurs when the brain misunderstands something seen by the eyes. Study these pictures and you may be deceived by your own eyes.

What is a mirage?

An optical illusion caused by light rays bending in heat or cold. An object over the horizon can be seen in the sky.

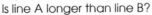

Are these two black faces or one white candlestick?

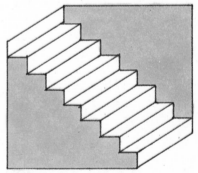

Is this flight of steps seen from above or below?

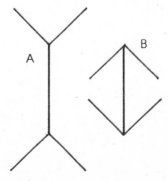

Is line A longer than line B?

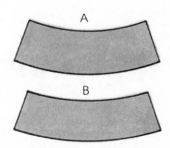

Is the top shape A bigger than the bottom shape B?

How wild was the West?

When the United States gained independence in 1783, only the eastern side of the country, up to the Mississippi River was explored. Soon daring men such as trappers, adventurers and gold miners began spreading west. The only law they recognised was the law of the gun!

What were wagon trains?

Rumours began to reach the eastern states of the great rich lands of the West. Stories of great rivers, plentiful supplies of food and gold made families decide to risk everything. They sold their homes and packed everything into a small covered wagon.

Because of the risk from Indians and robbers they travelled in large numbers called wagon trains.

Who were the mountain men?

These were the tough men who blazed the trails across America. Bearded and dressed in skins they were mainly beaver trappers. Because of their knowledge of the country, many became guides for the wagon trains.

How do you get gold from a river?

Small pieces of gold get washed down the rivers and collect in quiet pools. People would scoop up the sand from the river and swirl it around in a shallow pan. The heavier pieces of gold would be left at the bottom.

What was the pony express?

This was a way of carrying mail and news almost 3,200km (2,000 miles) across America. Riders would race at top speed for up to 32km (20 miles) then change horses and race on again. When they were exhausted another rider would take over. This famous service lasted less than two years before the telegraph took over.

Who were the cowboys?

As the population of the United States grew and settled into towns, cattle were needed to feed the people. Huge herds of half-wild longhorn cattle had to be looked after, rounded up and taken long distances to the railroad stations. This was the job of the cowboy.

Did cowboys carry guns?

Cowboys faced many dangers. Indians and cattle-rustlers would try to steal the herd, and animals such as bears, wolves and mountain lions preyed on the cattle and the cowboys. So every man would carry a revolver and a rifle.

What is a lariat?

It is a cowboy's rope. When a cow needed to be picked out from the herd, the cowboy would throw his rope over its head and quickly tie the other end to the saddle horn. The lariat would be about 10m (32ft) in length.

What are chaps?

The name comes from the Mexican word 'chaparejos'. They are heavy leather leg protectors.

If the cowboy had to chase cattle into rough bush country his legs would get badly cut. Chaps also protected him from the horns of the cattle.

What is a cowboy's hat called?

The large wide-brimmed hats were nicknamed ten gallon hats. The proper name was a stetson, after the hat maker who designed them.

What is cattle branding?

Because the cattle roamed freely over large areas of land, the owners had to mark their own animals. They did this by burning a design into the hide. The cattle had very tough hide so this did not hurt.

Were there really outlaws?

Because of the huge size of the American West, and the small number of law officers, it was easy for criminals to avoid capture.

Famous characters included Butch Cassidy and the Sundance Kid, and the woman cattle rustler, Belle Starr.

Butch Cassidy   The Sundance Kid

SHERIFF

Who was Davy Crockett?

He was a hunter and a politician. Texas once belonged to Mexico, but the American rulers fought against the Mexican ruler Santa Anna. Davy Crockett died at the battle of the Alamo.

What was the iron horse?

It was the name the Indians gave to the train. The railroad began to spread across America after the civil war ended in 1865. The Indians hated the railroad because it crossed their hunting ground.

Did you know the Union Jack was really three flags in one?

The English red cross of St George was combined with the Scottish flag of St Andrew in 1606. The Irish flag of St Patrick was included in 1800. Union Jack is the name given to the flag after the three flags were unified.

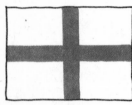
St George

St Andrew

St Patrick

What do the stars and stripes mean?

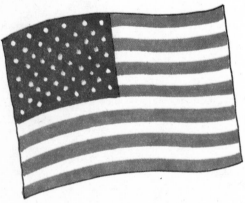

The flag of the United States of America is also nicknamed 'the stars and stripes'. The 13 stripes represent the 13 states that declared their independence in 1776. As new states joined the union, the flag changed 26 times. The 50 white stars represent the number of states in the whole of the union. The USA's anthem is the Star Spangled Banner.

What are decibels?

A decibel (db) is a unit for measuring the loudness or intensity of sound. Whispering is 20db, speaking is 60db. The scale increases in units - a sound measured at 50db is ten decibels louder than one of 40db.

Long exposure to sounds of over 120db (a disco or rock concert) can damage hearing.

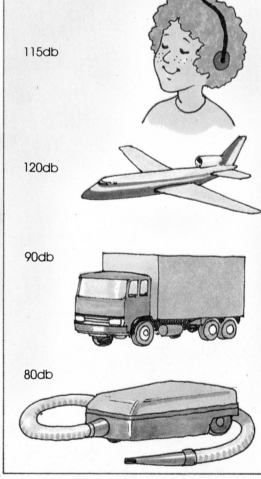

115db

120db

90db

80db

Did unicorns ever exist?

The unicorn was a mythical beast that for centuries was believed to exist. The horse with a single horn in the middle of its head was used on coats of arms. Even today it is still a popular design symbol.

In the past people finding the long spiralled tusk of the narwal (sea unicorn) might have thought it belonged to a unicorn.

What bird is called a bone-breaker?

The lammergeier vulture or bone-breaker has a unique way of getting at its food. It drops bones from a height down onto a rocky surface, then flys down to eat the bone marrow. Vultures often drop eggs, shellfish and sometimes tortoises in the same way.

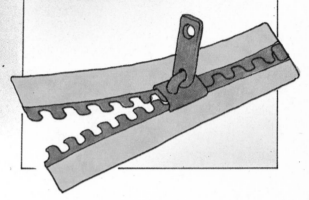

Who invented the zip fastener?

The zip fastener or zipper with small interlocking teeth was invented back in 1890 by American Whitecomb Judson. It took about 20 years before his invention was satisfactory. The zip was first used on snow boots.

What is an airship?

An airship is a sausage-shaped balloon filled with a lighter-than-air gas that makes it float. The early airships could carry passengers across the Atlantic, but they were slow and dangerous because they were filled with hydrogen gas which burns easily. Modern airships are filled with safe helium gas, but they are still slow.

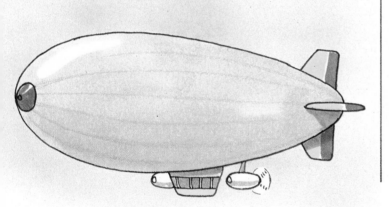

When was food first put in cans?

Food in tin cans was first produced in Britain in 1812 by Donkin and Hall of London. They canned beef, mutton, vegetable stew, soups and carrots. These goods were very useful to the explorers of the day.

An early can opener

Can you stay warm in an igloo?

You can. The Eskimo igloo is a temporary home used on hunting trips. It is built by cutting large blocks of hard packed snow and placing them one on top of another to form a dome shaped house. Fur rugs are spread on the floor. Light and warmth come from a small lamp that burns seal oil.

What were mammoths?

They were hairy elephant-like mammals that stood 4.5m (14ft 9in) high. They lived in herds and roamed across northern Europe, Asia and North America during the Ice Age.

Remains of these huge animals have been found in great numbers in places such as Siberia. Often their bodies have been found completely intact, as though they died recently. This is because the sub-zero temperatures prevented their flesh from deteriorating.

Does a skunk smell so bad?

Not only does a skunk smell bad, its spray can cause choking, and it can sting the eyes, causing temporary blindness. A skunk turns, raises its tail and squirts spray up to 3.5m (11ft 6in) from a gland beneath its tail.

What is an electric eel?

It's not an eel at all, but a freshwater fish, measuring up to 1.8m (6ft) long and related to the carp. The electric eel, which swims in the lakes and rivers of South America, can kill a human being as it releases a powerful 500 volt shock from electric organs in its body.

Who was St Francis of Assisi?

He was born in the hillside town of Assisi, Italy in 1182. St Francis is the patron saint of animals, and he founded the order of Franciscans.

He led a wild life in his youth, then he changed - he took a vow of poverty, helped those in need and preached the Christian gospel.

Is the Red Sea red?

The Red Sea owes its name to an algae that gives a red tinge to the water. This narrow inland sea is a branch of the Indian Ocean between north east Africa and the Arabian peninsula.

What is the Dead Sea?

It is a lake 369m (1,299ft) below sea level on the Israel/Jordan border. The water is seven times more salty than sea water. No fish can live in this water and swimmers float, but cannot sink.

How fast is a sneeze?

When something irritates the nerve endings of your nose you take a deep breath and sneeze at over 160km/h (100mph). Bless you!

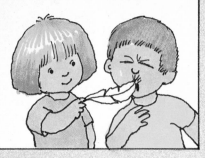

Who invented jeans?

A sailmaker, Oscar Levi-Strauss, in San Francisco in 1850. The word 'jeans' may come from 'jene fustien', a strong twill cotton cloth, first made in Genoa. The original jeans were brown until blue denim was used.

Who was Madame Tussaud?

She was a French woman who made wax images from the death masks of royalty and aristocrats who had been beheaded by the guillotine during the French revolution.

The collection of wax works was founded in 1770 and brought to England in 1802. It has had a permanent home in London since 1835.

Was there a real Count Dracula?

Bram Stoker's novel about Dracula has been popular ever since 1897. Through films, plays, even comic books, everyone is familiar with Count Dracula, the bloodsucking vampire. The original Dracula may have been the 15th century prince Vlad Tepes. He was an evil, cruel man, but certainly not a vampire.

What is Transylvania?

In Romania, Transylvania is a wild rocky region in the Carpathian mountains. It covers an area of 55,166 sq. km (21,300 sq. miles).

What does the word 'Eskimo' mean?

The people of the Arctic are called Eskimo, which means 'eating it raw'.

Traditionally, they lived on a diet of raw fish, walrus, seal blubber and whale skin.

They prefer to call themselves 'Inuit', which means 'the people'.

Do peanuts grow on trees?

Peanuts (or ground nuts) are the seeds of a plant. The flower stalks bend over, bury themselves in the soil and the pods ripen underground.

Can you bake Alaska?

This delicious dessert of ice cream on a cake base surrounded by meringue, then baked, was put together by New York chef, Charles Rahofer. This special sweet was to celebrate the American purchase of Alaska in 1867 from the Russians.

Which US president was a peanut farmer?

Jimmy Carter, the 39th President of the USA, was a naval officer and peanut farmer from Plains, Georgia.

What is the sound barrier?

As an aircraft flys it sends forward a pressure wave at the speed of sound.

If the plane flies at the same speed a shock wave of sound is produced called the 'sonic boom'.

What is an Oscar?

Oscar is the nickname of the golden statuette presented to people in the film industry for their work.

The Oscar ceremony is a glittering occasion with several Oscars being won annually.

The first of these trophies was presented in 1929. Four years later someone jokingly remarked that the statue looked like her Uncle Oscar - that name has been used ever since.

Was chewing gum invented in America?

Chewing gum was popular with the Mayans centuries ago. These central Americans chewed a gum-like latex from the chicle tree. Gum first came to the United States in 1860 and was flavoured with mint and aniseed.

What is the yeti?

Some people claim to have seen the yeti, a tall ape-like creature that is said to live high up in the Himalayas. Strange tracks found in the snow may belong to this animal, commonly known as the 'abominable snowman'.

Why does a candle burn?

When you light the wick of a candle the heat melts the wax and it creeps up the wick. As it meets the flame, wax vapour forms, mixes with oxygen in the air and burns!

Did you know that your body is two thirds water?

Every part of our body contains water. The weight of the adult human is made up of between 65 and 70% water, which is around 45 litres (79 pints).

Where were fireworks invented?

The Chinese had firework displays back in the 9th century. They used black gunpowder, a mixture of saltpetre, charcoal and sulphur. They fired rockets on very special occasions.

Which bird can smell with its beak?

The kiwi from New Zealand has nostrils at the tip of its beak. It sniffs out insects and worms and then pecks them out of the earth with its long beak.

Why is the sea salty?

Salt is a mineral that is gradually washed out of the rocks by rain and runs into the sea, making it taste salty. When sea water evaporates, salt is left behind.

What is the difference between a longbow and a crossbow?

The longbow is an ancient weapon. Originally made from one piece of wood, it could shoot an arrow over a long distance, making hunting much easier.

The crossbow is a small powerful bow, held and fired like a rifle. As a weapon of war it was deadly - it could pierce armour, but it was slow to reload.

Do you know what a totem pole is?

Among some Indians, certain creatures are believed to be the ancestors of the tribe. Totem animals are elaborately carved and painted on great wooden poles, often depicting the legends or exploits of the people.

What are pearls?

If a tiny grain of sand or grit gets inside an oyster, the creature protects itself by building a series of layers around the grain. The substance that forms these layers hardens to form a pearl.

What is amber?

It is fossilised resin from conifer trees that seeped out millions of years ago. Often insects were trapped inside. It lies buried until it is washed up on the seashore.

What is a pangolin?

A nocturnal scaly anteater. Most of its body is covered in yellow-brown scales. It rolls up like a ball and lives on ants and termites.

What is a geyser?

A hot spring that shoots a column of water and steam up into the air every so often. In volcanic regions water collects in deep cracks in the earth. It is heated by hot rocks and turns into steam that erupts with great force.

What is a shooting star?

It is really a meteor. Tiny rock particles flare up as they meet the atmosphere. They shoot across the sky, visible for a few seconds, then usually burn up.

Does a roadrunner really run?

Although the roadrunner can fly, it takes off at great speed to catch lizards and snakes, often running down the road. The roadrunner lives in the deserts of the USA and Mexico.

How did the leotard get its name?

This body-hugging garment worn by dancers and gymnasts was designed by Jules Leotard, a French trapeze artiste of the 1860s.

How does the flying fish fly?

This fish cannot fly like a bird, but it leaps into the air, up to 6m (20ft) then glides for about 400m (1,300ft) before splashing back.

Who built St Paul's Cathedral?

When he died in 1723 at the age of 90, Sir Christopher Wren had designed 50 churches in the city of London. His finest building was St Paul's Cathedral, which he built after the great fire of London.

The work began in 1675 and took 35 years to complete. The final stone was laid by Wren's son in 1710.

How much did St Paul's cost?

The total cost was £850,000. It was paid for by taxing all the boat loads of coal that arrived in the Port of London.

Where is the whispering gallery?

A gallery runs around the interior of the great dome of St Paul's. If you whisper inside this gallery your voice can be heard clearly on the opposite side, 34m (112ft) away.

Where is the Wren Memorial?

Above Wren's tomb in St. Paul's are written these words, "Reader, if you seek his monument, look about you!"

When was the great fire?

It began early in the morning of Sunday September 2nd 1666, at the house of a baker in Pudding Lane. The fire burned for three days, devastating the city of London. Many houses were built of wood, so the fire spread rapidly. In the end gunpowder was used to blow up some streets, producing gaps too wide for the flames to leap across. By this time, 460 streets had been destroyed, nearly 90 churches and 13,000 houses.

What is the Tower of London?

A fortress on the bank of the Thames. The oldest part is the keep or the White Tower, built in 1078 by William the Conqueror on the site of an earlier Roman fortress. For centuries it was used as a royal residence and a state prison.

Which treasure is kept in the Tower?

The Crown jewels or regalia, used by the King or Queen on state occasions, are kept in vaults under the Waterloo Barracks. They include eight crowns, sceptres, orbs and the coronation ring. The imperial state crown has nearly 3,000 diamonds.

Some of the Crown jewels of Great Britain

Why are ravens kept there?

According to legend, Britain will be invaded if the ravens leave the Tower. Charles II passed a royal charter ordering at least six ravens to be kept there at all times.

Who are the beefeaters?

The yeoman warders or beefeaters (French word, 'boufitiers', guardians of the king's buffet) were formed in 1485 by Henry VII. There are about 40 of them living and working in the Tower.

How old are the first human footprints?

They were made 3.75 million years ago by a group of early human-like creatures as they walked across a strip of volcanic ash near the Olduvai Gorge in Tanzania, Africa. The ash dried and became hard, which preserved the footprints until they were found in 1976.

Do turtles have teeth?

Turtles and tortoises do not have teeth. Their jaws have razor-sharp edges to cut up and shred their food.

What is a loofah?

The bathroom loofah is the dried centre of a vegetable called the luffa.

It is a member of the gourd family of plants and related to the pumpkin and the cucumber.

Who is Nanook?

The Eskimos call the polar bear 'Nanook', which means 'ice-bear'. These huge bears that roam the Arctic often weigh up to 600kg (1,323lb) and stand around 3.5m (11.5ft) tall.

Who launched the first satellite?

On October 4th 1957, Russia launched the first man-made satellite into space. It was known as Sputnik-1. The satellite was a sphere 56cm (22in) in diameter and weighed 83.6kg (185lb).

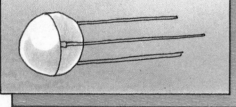

Who played golf on the Moon?

US astronaut Alan Shepherd, the commander of Apollo14, played the first golf shot on the Moon in 1971.

Who went for the first drive on the Moon?

On July 31st 1971, astronauts David Scott and James Irwin (two of the crew of Apollo 15) drove for several miles across the bumpy surface of the Moon. They rode in their lunar roving vehicle or 'moon buggy'

How much honey comes from a hive?

An average colony of bees in a hive (about 60,000 worker bees) can produce around 25kg (1lb) of pure honey in a year.

Do all bees sting?

Only female bees can sting. A bee's sting is like a sharp thorn at the end of its abdomen. If the thorn is left in your flesh, the bee cannot sting again!

What happened to King Midas?

In Greek mythology, Midas was granted a wish by the god Dionysus. Midas asked that everything he touched should turn to gold.

At first it was wonderful, but when he reached for food and drink, and that turned to gold, he soon began to starve. When he touched his beloved daughter and she turned to gold too, he begged for his wish to be taken back!

What is Reuters?

It is an organisation whose agents supply newspapers with news from all over the world. It was founded in Germany in 1849 by a man named Reuter. At first he sent his messages by pigeon post until the telegraph was invented.

What is an ermine?

In cold climates the red-brown fur of the stoat turns white in winter. It is then known as an ermine. The white fur with its distinctive black-tipped tail is used on some ceremonial robes.

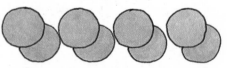

Which animal can sleep on its back?

Humans are the only animals that can do this!

How is a watermark made?

When paper is made, wet pulp is spread on fine wire gauze to dry. Some of the wires can be arranged to form words or designs that appear on the paper as a watermark. Hold the paper up to the light and see!

What does G.M.T. stand for?

G.M.T. is short for Greenwich Mean Time. It is the scientific standard of time for the whole world. The BBC broadcast the Greenwich time signal on the radio. Every hour, on the hour, you can count the six bleeps or 'pips'. The last pip sounds exactly on the hour!

Who was Neptune?

He was the Roman god of the sea. To the Greeks he was known as Poseidon. With his three-pronged trident he is said to control the wind and the waves.

Who rode in the first hot-air balloon?

Before the French Montgolfier brothers made their first manned flight in a hot-air balloon in 1783, they sent a duck, a cock and a sheep up first. They wanted to find out if the animals would be harmed by the thinner air.

What shook San Francisco?

In April 1906, a great earthquake and fire destroyed over a third of the city. Over 100,000 people were made homeless in the 30-second tremor. San Francisco is built on the San Andreas Fault, so this could happen any time!

Do birds have teeth?

No they don't. The structure of birds' bodies must be light. Strong jaw bones and teeth would add weight to a bird's skull and this would make flying difficult.

When did the first birds live on Earth?

About 150 million years ago there lived a bird-like creature called an archaeopteryx. It had feathers, wings and a head like a lizard with sharp teeth instead of a beak. It was about as big as a seagull.

What is the best way to keep warm?

Wear several layers of clothing. Air is trapped between the layers, and this helps you to keep warm.

Who founded the Boy Scouts?

The Scout movement was formed by Lord Baden-Powell, whose book *Scouting for Boys* appeared in 1908. This movement has spread throughout the world.

Lord Baden-Powell and his sister founded the Girl Guide organisation in 1910.

Is a mole blind?

A mole has very poor eyesight, but is not blind. Its tiny eyes are hidden deep in its fur.

The mole burrows under the surface of the ground in search of worms and insects. It has a huge appetite and cannot live for more than 12 hours without food.

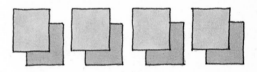

How did we get the word 'alphabet'?

From the first two letters of the Greek alphabet, 'alpha' and 'beta'.

What creature hides behind a trap-door?

The trap-door spider digs a tunnel and covers it with a trap-door. It hides underneath with the trap-door slightly open. When its prey comes along it jumps out and grabs it!

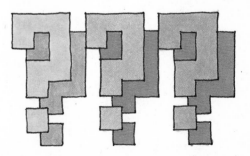

What is the Colosseum?

A great amphitheatre in Rome completed in AD80. It was a huge stadium for chariot races, gladiator fighting and even mock sea battles. The Romans enjoyed games in which people and wild animals were killed in the most cruel ways. Admission was free even to slaves. There were seats for more than 80,000 people and standing room for 20,000 more.

The Colosseum is now in ruins and is one of the sights of Rome.

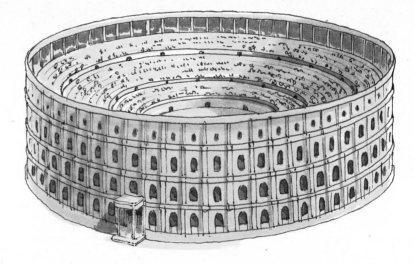

Who were the gladiators?

They were men who fought in the arena to entertain the ancient Romans. Usually they were slaves, prisoners of war or criminals - a few were volunteers.

There were different kinds of gladiators. Some wore armour with helmets and shields, and fought with a sword or an axe; some were armed with a trident and a net; others used a noose.

Most contests were fought to the death, but gladiators who survived many battles became heroes and retired as wealthy men.

When the defeated gladiator was not killed during a fight, it was the custom for the crowd to signal with their thumbs whether his life should be spared. Thumbs up meant that he should live; thumbs down meant that he should die.

Who were the samurai?

The samurai were the old warrior class of Japan. From an early age children were taught to fight using a curved two-handed sword called a katana. Each warrior also carried a smaller sword called a wakizashi. Their other main weapon was the longbow.

These fierce warriors were also trained in artistic skills such as poetry, writing and flower arranging!

What was their armour made of?

Suits of armour with great helmets were mainly ceremonial. The fighting man wore lightweight armour made of small metal plates fastened together with coloured cards.

What was a shogun?

The shogun was the military ruler of old Japan. Japan was always ruled by emperors who claimed to be descended from the gods. But as the samurai lords became more powerful, the emperors became more of a religious figurehead. The real power in the land was held by the strongest of the samurai leaders who took the title of shogun.

Do the samurai still exist?

Japan remained an almost closed country living in the past, until 1854 when a treaty was signed with the United States. After that the samurai had no real place in Japan and ended in 1877.

Which famous skyscraper did King Kong climb?

It was the Empire State Building in New York, a skyscraper office block completed in 1931. For 40 years this 102 storey, 381m (1,250ft) high building was the tallest in the world. From the top you can see for 130km (80miles).

In the film *King Kong* (1933) the citizens of New York were terrorised by a huge ape that climbed to the top of the skyscraper and was finally shot down by US army fighter planes.

Who was the first man in space?

The Russian major Yuri Alexeyevitch Gagarin became the first man to fly in space on April 12th 1961. His spaceship Vostock orbited the Earth for 108 minutes before returning.

He was killed at the age of 34 in 1968 when the MIG-15 jet trainer he was flying crashed.

What is mistletoe?

This evergreen plant is a parasite, growing on the branches of various forest and fruit trees. Mistletoe was sacred to the people of ancient Europe. Druids used it in their sacrifices and the Celts believed it had magical and healing powers.

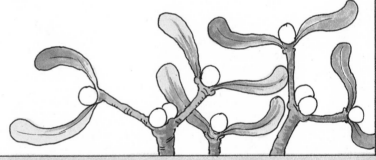

What is the Bayeaux Tapestry?

It is an embroidery, commissioned for Bayeaux Cathedral in Calvados, France. It shows the conquest of England by the Norman King, William I in 1066.

It is worked in eight colours on a band of linen 70.4m (231ft) long, and 50cm (20in) deep.

The story of the Norman invasion is told in 72 scenes, starting with the English King Harold's visit to the Norman Court and ending with his death at Hastings, shot through the eye by an arrow.

The tapestry can still be seen at Bayeaux.

What is the world's highest mountain?

Mount Everest at 8,848m (29,028ft) is the highest mountain above sea level.

The island of Hawaii, however, is the top of a mountain, Mauna Kea, which is 9,150m (30,000ft) high from its undersea base.

How does a squid get out of trouble?

When danger threatens, the squid, like the octopus and the cuttlefish, can squirt dark ink fluid to conceal themselves. The ink clouds the water and confuses their enemy.

Where does ice cream come from?

The Romans ate ices of fruit juice and wine added to snow. The explorer Marco Polo returned to Venice from the Orient in 1295 with recipes for ice cream made with milk.

What is the Chinese magic square?

'Magic' squares have fascinated scientists for hundreds of years. This is one of the earliest from China, written down in 12BC. Each row, each column and both diagonals add up to 15!

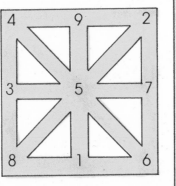

What is a vacuum?

A space that contains absolutely nothing! Scientists believe that it is impossible to have a complete vacuum - an empty space with no air or substance whatsoever.

So a vacuum as we know it, is an enclosed space from which as much air and matter as possible has been removed.

A thermos flask has a double wall inside, with a vacuum between the two walls. Hot liquid is kept hot because the heat cannot pass through the vacuum by convection or conduction.

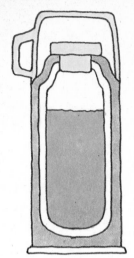

What is shorthand?

Shorthand is a quick way of writing. Words are represented by simple strokes and symbols.

Early shorthand was first used in 63BC. Modern shorthand was invented by Pitman in 1837 and a system devised by Gregg has been in use in America since 1888.

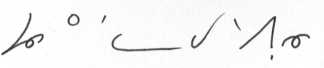

Which bird catches fish for people to eat?

A web-footed diving bird, the cormorant, with a huge appetite for fish. In the East, fishermen use the cormorant to dive underwater to catch fish for them. A metal ring around the bird's neck stops it from swallowing the fish.

How can cats see in the dark?

No animal can see in total darkness, but when the light is poor, cats can enlarge (dilate) the pupils of their eyes. This means that more light is admitted to the eye.

Owls use this technique as well.

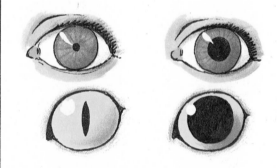

How much of the world's natural water is in the oceans?

Water is nature's most plentiful liquid.

Three quarters of the Earth is covered in it, and 97% of all the world's water flows in the oceans. The polar ice caps hold another 2% and the remainder goes round and round in the world's water cycle forever, evaporating and falling again as rain or snow.

Why do animals' eyes shine in the dark?

Many animals have a layer of crystalline substance in their eyes that reflects light. When their eyes shine it is just the reflection of other lights, a car's headlights or perhaps the street lights.

Which US president was born in a log cabin?

Abraham Lincoln, the 16th president of the USA was born on February 16th 1809 in a log cabin on the Kentucky frontier. Lincoln grew up on a farm in Indiana. He educated himself and became a lawyer, and in 1861 he was elected president.

What is an illuminated manuscript?

Before the invention of printing, all books were copied by hand. Monks and scribes laboriously wrote out the text in pen on parchment. Often single letters, words and borders were decorated or illuminated in these manuscripts.

When was dormouse on the menu?

The Romans really did eat dormice! They were stuffed with minced pork, pepper, pine kernels and garlic, placed on a tile and baked in the oven. The recipe dates back to the first century BC.

Which country does this flag belong to?

It is not one country's flag, but the flag of the European Community. No one could decide on a new flag for Europe, so in 1986 the EC adopted the Council of Europe's flag.

Who ate their plates at dinner time?

In the Middle Ages you could eat your plate if you were really hungry, because it was a thick slice of unleavened bread. Usually it was given to the poor or the dogs at the end of a meal.

Which great musician was deaf?

Ludwig Van Beethoven, born in Bonn in 1790, was one of the world's greatest composers. He began to lose his hearing at the age of 26, and by 1823 he was completely deaf. Beethoven never heard his nine symphonies or piano concertos, or any of his other compositions during the last ten years of his life.

Where is Poet's Corner?

It is in the south transept of Westminster Abbey. In 1956 a monument was erected there to Geoffrey Chaucer (1340-1400), one of the first poets to write in the English language. His poems *The Canterbury Tales* are about a band of pilgrims who travel from London to the shrine of Thomas à Becket at Canterbury. During their pilgrimage each traveller tells a story. Since Chaucer it has been a great honour for a poet to be commemorated in Poet's Corner.

Who is buried there?

Few poets are actually buried in the abbey, but Chaucer, Shakespeare, Milton, Wordsworth, Keats, Shelley and Ben Jonson are remembered in Poet's Corner.

Who was Icarus?

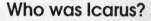

In Greek mythology, Icarus and his father Daedalus tried to escape from the island of Crete by flying away on wings made of feathers and wax. Icarus flew too close to the Sun, the wax melted and he plunged into the Aegean sea and drowned.

Why do we blush?

When our cheeks go red with embarrassment, shame, or even pleasure, people say we are blushing!

Tiny blood vessels (capillaries) under the skin open wide to let lots of blood run through. Blushing is one of the ways the body has for keeping the blood it sends to the brain at the correct temperature.

Why do we turn pale when frightened?

Your face turns white because blood is diverted to another part of your body. The heart pumps faster and stronger pushing blood to the limb muscles and adrenaline is released into the bloodstream. In fact, your body is getting itself ready to run or even fight.

When danger is past the body quickly returns to normal.

Who was Ned Kelly?

He was a famous Australian bandit or bushranger, the leader of the outlawed Kelly gang. Although he was a bank robber and defied the police for years, Ned Kelly was admired and thought of as a hero!

He wore strange iron armour made from a plough share. In 1880 he was finally captured and his gang were killed. Later Kelly was hanged and became a legend.

Is a sea anemone a plant?

No, it is an animal that attaches itself to rocks. The anemone seizes and paralyses shrimps and shellfish with its waving tentacles before pulling them into its mouth to be digested.

Which crab lives in a borrowed shell?

Hermit crabs use abandoned mollusc shells as homes. This crab's abdomen is soft, so the extra shell is for protection. When the crab grows it simply finds a bigger shell to live in.

Who built the Taj Mahal?

The Mogul emperor Shah Jahan had one of the most beautiful buildings in the world built at Agra in India, as a tomb for his beloved wife Mumtaz Mahal. She had 14 children and died when she was 39.

From 1630, over a period of 20 years, 20,000 men worked on the white marble tomb. The walls were inlaid with 12 different kinds of semi-precious stones and carved inscriptions from the Koran.

Today people can visit the Taj Mahal between the hours of dawn and dusk. It is just outside the city of Delhi in northern India.

What happened to Shah Jahan?

Shah Jahan was born in 1592 and died in 1666. He became emperor in 1628 and during his reign some of the finest monuments of Mogul architecture were built.

When Shah Jahan had finished building his wife's tomb, he planned to build an identical one in black marble for himself. It was to stand on the opposite bank of the River Jumna from the Taj Mahal, connected by a silver bridge.

Sadly, his own son imprisoned him in this palace before it was complete and the Indian emperor died there. Now his tomb lies in the Taj Mahal beside his wife Mumtaz.

Which American presidents are carved into a mountain?

In the Black Hills of Dakota, USA, is the site of Mount Rushmore National Memorial, covering 13 sq. km (5 sq. miles). These giant heads took Gutzon Borglum 15 years to carve out of the face of the mountain. They represent four American presidents: Washington, Jefferson, Lincoln and Theodore Roosevelt. The heads from chin to top are 18m (60ft) high.

Which building looks like a sailing ship?

The white curved roof of the Sydney Opera House was designed to look like the billowing sails of a ship sailing in the waters of Sydney Harbour.

Danish architect Jorn Utzon won an international contest with his design for the Opera House and work began in 1957. It was completed 16 years later, having cost 14 times more than the original estimate. Most of the extra cash was raised by a series of Opera House lotteries.

If you visit the Opera House you must park and then take a bus for 1.6km (1 mile), as there is no car park!

Who were the Aztecs?

They were a race of Indians who were living in the plains of central and southern America.

The Aztecs were a wandering people until 1324 when they settled in a marshy village called Tenochtitlan. Legend says that it is the place where they found an eagle on a cactus eating a serpent, and that is where their gods told them to build a great city. Tenochtitlan grew into just that. As well as a magnificent city, the Aztecs built a great pyramid-shaped temple where they carried out hundreds of human sacrifices, cutting out the hearts as an offering to their gods.

But in 1519 the Spaniard, Cortés led an expedition into Mexico. In less than two years he had killed the Aztec leader Montezuma and destroyed their city. Cortés had better weapons, and soldiers mounted on horseback - the Aztecs were terrified, as they had never seen a horse before. Soon they were defeated and Mexico was claimed for Spain.

Today the Aztec city of Tenochtitlan lies beneath modern Mexico City. The Great Temple has been excavated and the site can be visited today.

The Aztec God
Quetzalcoatl

Who were the Incas?

This was the name of the people who lived in the mountains of Peru before the arrival of the Spaniards.

The Incas called themselves 'children of the Sun', which they worshipped as a god. They mined gold and silver and made it into beautiful statues, masks and ornaments. They built roads around the steep mountain sides, connecting them by rope and vine bridges. No vehicles ever used these routes, as the Incas did not have the wheel!

This great civilisation came to a swift end when the Spaniards came in search of land and gold. The Spanish conquistador, Pizarro, marched into Peru with 180 men and 37 horses to conquer the country. He captured the Inca ruler Atahualpa, and accepted a room full of gold for the ruler to be returned to his people. But after the Spaniards had taken the gold, they put Atahualpa to death.

Within a few years, the whole of the Inca empire and all its treasures belonged to Spain. Very few of the golden statues and ornaments can be seen today as the Spaniards melted them down into ingots.

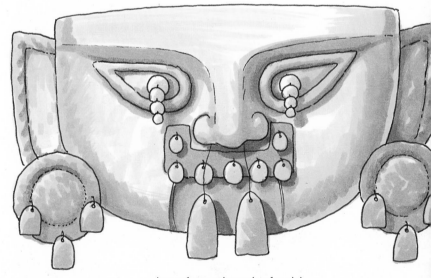

Inca funeral mask of gold

Can you see an Inca city today?

Machu Picchu is a ruined city that the Incas abandoned. It stands on a mountain ridge high in the south western Andes. This ancient city was undiscovered until 1911, when an American archaeologist, Hiram Bingham, was the first to see it.

If you ever travel to Peru, you can walk around the ruined houses and terraces of Machu Picchu.

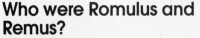

Who were Romulus and Remus?

They are part of a famous legend about the founding of Rome.

As babies, the twin boys Romulus and Remus were left in their cradle to drown in the River Tiber. They were rescued by a she-wolf and later found by a shepherd. When they grew up they decided to found a city, but quarrelled over the choice of site, and Remus was killed. When the city was built, Romulus named it Rome - after himself.

Who was Hercules?

He was a famous hero of Greek mythology. Hercules was well known for his great strength and courage. While still in his cradle, he strangled two serpents that were sent to kill him.

As the legend goes, when he became a man he was set 12 impossible tasks, known as the 12 labours. One of the tasks was to clean out the Augean stables, in which King Augeas had kept 3,000 cattle for 30 years. Hercules cleaned the stables in one day by diverting two rivers through them.

When all 12 of his tasks were finished, he set sail with Jason and the Argonauts to find the Golden Fleece.

After his death, because of his many brave adventures, Hercules became a god.

What was a minotaur?

In Greek mythology it was a monstrous creature that was half-man, half-bull. The minotaur was kept in the middle of a labyrinth or maze, by King Minos of Crete. Every year it killed seven young men and sent seven young women from Athens as a sacrifice.

One year a boy named Theseus volunteered to join the young men and try to kill the minotaur.

With the help of Ariadne (daughter of King Minos) he found his way into the maze, and bravely killed the monster.

He was able to find his way out of the labyrinth as Ariadne had given him a ball of thread to mark his path.

How talented was the young Mozart?

Little Wolfgang Amadeus Mozart could play the harpsichord at the age of three. He composed music at the age of five, and some of those tunes he wrote still survive today.

In 1762, when he was only six, he played in concerts in Munich and Vienna with his 11-year-old sister Maria Anna.

For the next few years the two children travelled all over Europe giving concerts, often in front of royalty.

When he was 21, the Austrian Emperor asked Mozart to write his first opera, and the Archbishop of Salzburg made the young boy leader of his court orchestra. By the time he was 15, he had already composed 13 symphonies. During his short lifetime he wrote over 600 works, but Mozart earned very little money from his music and was often in debt.

He died in 1791 at the age of 35. Mozart, who was probably the greatest musician that ever lived, was buried in an unmarked grave in St Mark's cemetery, Vienna.

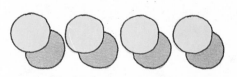

Can a bird fly all of the time?

Most birds fly for short periods and then return to land to rest and feed. There are some birds that can fly non-stop for years. The sooty tern flies over the oceans for 3-10 years before returning to land to breed.

Which bird builds an oven?

The oven bird gets its name from the strong, oven-shaped nest that it builds up from layers of mud.

Can birds fly backwards?

Humming birds can! These tiny birds with their high speed wing beats can fly in any direction, even backwards. They can also keep their bodies perfectly still in mid-air.

Which bird flies underwater?

On land the flightless penguin is a clumsy, funny creature. Underwater it 'flies' with great speed and grace.

Which bird has the largest wingspan?

The wandering albatross spends its life flying over the southern oceans. With its 3.5m (12ft) wingspan, it glides over the waves stopping only to feed.

Which bird goes to prison?

The female hornbill is sealed into her nest in a hollow made by the male. He does this to protect both her and the eggs from dangers such as monkeys.

What is bird's-nest soup?

This Chinese delicacy is made by soaking and cooking the nests of a type of swift. The bird makes its nest with saliva.

Which bird can weave?

The male red-headed weaverbird makes a large nest by weaving grasses together. These strong nests may last for a year and can be used many times.

Did you know that a bird can sew?

The tailorbird makes a nest using its sharp beak as a needle to sew two large leaves together. The leaves are then filled with soft grasses.

Did you know that the peregrine falcon can dive at over 320km/h (200mph)?

This is the fastest bird in flight, but it would not be able to dive on its prey at this speed.

Who was Genghis Khan?

The Mongol ruler who built up the vast Mongol empire in the early 1200s.

Genghis Khan and his armies terrorised people with their violence and cruelty, but to his people he was God's representative on Earth, their supreme ruler.

He formed armies of horsemen, and after many victories whole armies came to join him. His fierce Mongol soldiers conquered most of northern China by breaking through the Great Wall. His empire stretched right across Asia and into Eastern Europe and Russia.

Who invented dynamite and left his money to peace?

Alfred Nobel, a Swedish chemist, invented dynamite in 1867 and gelignite in 1875.

During his early experiments his laboratory blew up, killing Nobel's younger brother and four workers.

Nobel made a huge fortune out of the manufacture of explosives and left the biggest part of the money for annual awards called Nobel Prizes. The seven prizes are for physics, chemistry, economics, physiology or medicine, literature and peace.

Who was Harry Houdini?

His real name was Erik Weiss and he was the most famous escapologist of all time. He could escape from locked handcuffs, straitjackets, even sealed, underwater boxes.

What was the deepest ocean dive?

This took place in 1960 when three members of the US navy descended into the 10,916m (35,800ft) deep Marianas Trench in the Pacific. They made the dive in a bathyscaphe called 'Trieste'.

What is the difference between a tortoise and a terrapin?

The shell of a tortoise is heavier and more dome-shaped than the terrapin's. Neither reptiles have teeth, but their jaws are razor sharp.

A terrapin has a more streamlined shape than a tortoise. It can live in fresh water as well as on land. Some of them have slightly webbed feet.

How do parrots stay on their perches while they sleep?

A bird has tendons in its feet that go up into the leg. When it perches the tendons are pulled tight and this makes the bird's toes curl around the perch in a tight grasp.

Who was the first person to reach the South Pole?

In December 1911, the Norwegian explorer Roald Amundsen won the race to the South Pole with four men and their dog teams. They reached the pole 34 days ahead of Captain Scott, whose party all died on the way home.

Is there really a Loch Ness monster?

Underwater cameras, frogmen and even submarines have searched the 37km (23 miles) of Loch Ness in vain. In 1960 a few seconds of film recorded something travelling across the surface of the water. Could Nessie really be a survivor from prehistory?

Who invented cornflakes?

Will Keith Kellogg discovered cornflakes by accident in 1894. His brother was a doctor looking for a food that was easy for patients to digest. Will boiled a pan of wheat and from its contents thought up the idea of cornflakes.

What happened to the Titanic?

On April 5th 1912 the Titanic was on her maiden voyage to New York when disaster struck! This great ship, said to be unsinkable, struck an iceberg and sank within two and half hours. More than 1,500 passengers and crew were drowned in the north Atlantic's freezing waters. Only 712 survived.

The Titanic was hoping to win the Blue Riband for the fastest Atlantic crossing!

Which animal is a worldwide symbol?

The World Wildlife Fund (WWF) for nature campaigns to protect wildlife and habitats all over the world. Its symbol is the giant panda.

Where do pandas live?

In isolated parts of China, high up in the mountains. They are very rare, and live alone in areas of bamboo forest.

Why do some creatures become extinct?

When a species dies out it disappears forever. Humans are often responsible for hunting and killing some animals to extinction, like the passenger pigeon, the last of which died in a zoo.

Who invented the frisbee?

In 1871 an American pie maker called Mr Frisbee supplied Yale University with pies in tins. The students ate the pies and threw the cases at each other. In 1948 the first plastic frisbee appeared.

Why do falcons wear hoods?

In falconry the birds are trained to catch prey and bring it back to the handler.

The falcon is hooded so that it is not distracted as it perches on the gloved wrist of the falconer. When the hood is removed the bird takes off in search of game.

Does coffee grow on trees?

It grows on an evergreen shrub in hot climates. Two seeds or beans grow inside a red cherry-like fruit. These beans are roasted and then ground to make coffee.

What is an avalanche?

When a mass of snow builds up on a mountain and then begins to slip it falls rapidly down the mountainside.

Often the slightest sound or movement can send thousands of tonnes of snow crashing down. A large avalanche can bury everything in its path.

Did Robin Hood really live in Sherwood Forest?

This legendary hero was said to have lived in Sherwood Forest, Nottinghamshire during the reign of Richard I who was King from 1189-1199.

During this time, Richard the Lionheart was away from England on crusades in the holy land and neglected his duties as King. He left his brother Prince John in charge of the country who, together with the Sheriff of Nottingham, declared Robin Hood an outlaw.

According to legend, Robin then became the leader of an outlaw band dressed in Lincoln green and armed with longbows, who robbed the rich to help the poor.

From the 14th century onwards, tales and ballads of this popular hero began to appear, but no one has really been able to prove that Robin Hood existed.

Was St George English?

Since medieval times, St George's Day has been celebrated on April 23rd. Although St George is the patron saint of England, he is thought to have come from North America. He may have been a Roman soldier, put to death for his Christian faith around AD300.

Legend says that St George came riding into a land where the people were terrorised by a dragon. Its next victim was to be the King's daughter. As the dragon was about to devour her, St George attacked and killed it with an iron lance.

Tales of this mysterious knight spread, and he became the saint of the medieval crusaders as well as the patron saint of many places - Venice, Portugal, parts of Spain and England. His special flag is a red cross on a white background.

Did King Arthur ever rule Britain?

As a boy of 15, Arthur pulled out a sword embedded in a great anvil, when everyone else had failed. This test proved that he was the rightful King of England.

At his court in Camelot, Arthur ruled with his Queen Guinevere, advised by Merlin the magician. His knights were devoted to a life of chivalry and sat equally placed at the Round Table.

Throughout his life Arthur carried a magic sword, Excalibur, given to him by the Lady of the Lake. On his death the sword was thrown back into the lake, out of which an arm appeared, took the sword and vanished!

The legend may have been based on a British warrior who fought the Saxons after the Romans left. Camelot could be Winchester, and Cornwall is thought to be the home of the legends of King Arthur.

Why did the Pied Piper take the children of Hamelin?

In 1284 the town of Hamelin in Germany was plagued by rats.

One day an odd looking piper appeared offering to rid the town of rats, and the Mayor gladly agreed to pay him. As he played his pipe, the rats followed the stranger towards the river, where they fell in and drowned.

When the Piper asked for his fee, the Mayor refused. As the piper played once more, all the children of the town followed him, dancing towards Koppelberg mountain. An enormous cavern opened up, the children ran inside and were never seen again!

Who shot an apple on his son's head?

In Switzerland in the 13th century, the Austrian governor Gessler ordered everyone to salute a hat placed by him on a pole in the market square. William Tell refused and was ordered to split an apple placed on his son's head with one arrow - or be killed!

Tell succeeded, but said he had a second arrow ready to kill Gessler if he had missed the apple and killed his son. As a result he was imprisoned, but he later escaped, shot Gessler and became a hero.

What is the forbidden city?

The forbidden city is in Beijing (Peking). In 1421, the third emperor of the Ming dynasty laid out his imperial walled capital like a series of boxes one inside the other.

First came the outer city, then the inner city, next the imperial city and last of all the forbidden city. Ordinary people entered on pain of death. Nowadays it is open to ordinary tourists.

What is a centipede?

Centipedes' bodies are made up of many segments, each with one pair of legs. Although the word 'centipede' means 100 feet, some of these meat-eating creatures can have as little as 15 pairs of legs, or as many as 177 pairs.

And what is a millipede?

The millipede, like the centipede, is not an insect, nor does it have a thousand feet. It has a worm-like segmented body with up to 240 legs.

Young millipedes have only six legs but extra legs grow as they mature.

Why do we shiver?

When you are very cold you shiver uncontrollably! Your muscles shake all over because this is the body's way of warming you up.

What was the world's first postage stamp?

The Penny Black was first used in England in May 1840. Six million were printed in unperforated sheets of 240. Post Office staff had to cut the stamps into strips. It cost one penny to deliver a letter, whatever the distance.

V POSTAGE R
ONE PENNY
G   L

Who celebrates Thanksgiving Day?

This day falls on the last Thursday in November. It is an annual national holiday in the USA, a traditional thanksgiving for the year's harvest.

The first Thanksgiving was celebrated by the Pilgrim Fathers in 1621 and lasted three whole days. The settlers and their Indian friends ate wild turkey, geese, duck, lobsters, clams, oysters and popcorn.

Where do turkeys come from?

These large wild game birds come from the USA. Early European settlers almost wiped out the turkey in North America because it became one of their favourite foods.

Who was the messenger of the gods?

Mercury was the mythological messenger of the Roman gods, his Greek name was Hermes. He wore a winged hat and winged sandals and carried a herald's wand intertwined with snakes or ribbon.

What is a secretary bird?

This African bird gets its name from the long feathers on its head, which resemble old fashioned quill pens. It runs swiftly after snakes, and kills them with its powerful legs.

Who first made paper?

Paper was first made by wasps! They make paper for their nests by chewing up fragments of wood.

The ancient Egyptians made paper from a water reed called papyrus - hence the name paper.

As early as the second century the Chinese manufactured paper from bamboo fibres, pounded and pulped and then left to dry.

Who invented frozen food?

Throughout history people living in sub-zero temperatures have always preserved their food by leaving it outside until it was frozen solid.

It wasn't until 1924 that food was frozen commercially. An American scientist named Clarence Birdseye went on an expedition to Labrador. He noticed fish and venison being eaten by the Eskimos. When thawed, cooked and eaten, the food lost none of its taste.

Back in America, Birdseye discovered a mechanical method of quick-freezing food. But it was very slow and he could freeze no more than 500 tonnes of fruit and vegetables a year.

Over the next few years he improved his freezing machinery, and on June 6th 1930, a group of Massachusetts' grocers offered boxes of frozen peas for sale!

When was Coca-Cola first tasted?

This world famous drink was invented over a hundred years ago by John Pemberton, a chemist from Atlanta, Georgia.

In 1886 he made up a syrup of cola-nut extract, caffeine, cocoa leaves, vegetable extracts and sugar.

One day his assistant diluted some of this syrup with soda-water, then served it to a customer in Pemberton's drugstore. This was the first Coca-Cola ever tasted.

The famous Coca-Cola trademark was originally the beautiful handwriting of Pemberton's business partner Frank Robertson.

How did the St Bernard dog get its name?

These huge, strong dogs were originally from the Swiss Alps. They were trained to dig out travellers lost or buried in snowdrifts as they crossed mountain passes.

It is a popular belief that the small barrel of brandy round the St Bernard's neck, was to revive any freezing survivors that the dogs might rescue. However, it was Sir Edwin Landseer (Queen Victoria's favourite artist) who added the barrel to one of his paintings, and people have believed the story ever since!

What is the Victoria Cross?

The highest British decoration for bravery by members of the armed services during a war. It was first instituted by Queen Victoria at the end of the Crimean War.

The medal is a Maltese Cross in bronze and for many years was made from cannon captured at Sevastopol.

What is the Purple Heart?

Since 1932, American servicemen wounded in battle have often received the Purple Heart, but it was back in 1782 that George Washington first introduced this award. Then, soldiers who displayed 'gallantry and faith' could stitch a purple heart-shaped patch of cloth onto their uniform.

For a hundred and fifty years this award was forgotten. Then it was revived in the 1930s!

How old is Mr Punch?

Mr Punch is thought to originate from an old Italian puppet called Pulcinella, first created around 1600 by Silvio Fiorillo, a comedian.

In 1662 Samuel Pepys saw Punchinello (later shortened to Punch) in London's Covent Garden for the first time. He wrote in his famous diary on May 9th that the puppet show was wonderful.

Punch and Judy shows were very popular in Victorian times. Charles Dickens mentions them in four of his novels.

In France Mr Punch is known as Polichinelle, and in Russia he is called Petrushka.

How did the piano get its name?

In 1710 the Italian, Bartolomeo Cristofori created the first pianoforte. Its name comes from two Italian words, 'piano' ('soft') and 'forte' ('loud').

Earlier instruments like the harpsichord had quills that plucked the strings when the keys were played, but the volume of the notes was the same.

On the new pianoforte, strings of different lengths were struck with felt-covered hammers. Hit the note hard and the hammer would make a louder note, touch the note gently and the music would play softly!

A piano can make notes of different volume according to the force with which the keys are struck.

Who were the first people to keep cats?

The ancient Egyptians kept cats more than 4,000 years ago. Their goddess Bastet was shown as a cat or cat-headed woman. To them, the cat was a sacred animal. Killing a cat, even by accident, was punishable by death!

If a pet cat died, the whole family would shave off their eyebrows as a sign of mourning. The Egyptians mummified their cats and buried them in special vaults, often with mummified mice!

Does milk come from cows?

Milk is one of our most complete foods, and one of the most important foods worldwide, but not all of it comes from cows!

Goats' milk is more easily digested than cows' milk. Water-buffalo milk is very rich. Ewes' milk is used in France to make Roquefort cheese. In Tibet they drink yaks' milk, and in Lapland reindeers' milk. Arabs milk their camels and Mongolians drink mares' milk.

Does milk come from trees?

Coconuts have a double shell and inside the inner rough brown shell of a fresh coconut you will find a sweet milk. If you pierce the 'eyes' of the nut with a skewer, you can drain the liquid into a bowl ready to drink!

Who first played the game of baseball?

The American game of baseball almost certainly came from England many years ago.

It was mentioned in 1700, when a vicar in Kent wrote how much he hated the game being played on a Sunday!

In one of Jane Austen's novels of 1798, she wrote that one of her characters preferred cricket, baseball and horse-riding to reading books!

In England, hundreds of years before this, children enjoyed playing rounders - a game very similar to baseball. When the first English colonists came to settle in America in the 1660s, they may have brought rounders with them - which eventually became baseball!

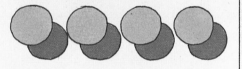

Can crabs climb trees?

The robber crab can easily climb up the trunks of coconut palms by gripping with its powerful pincers. It strips off the coconuts so they fall to the ground, ready for the crab to eat.

These tree-climbing crustaceans live on the tropical islands in the Pacific and Indian Oceans, and are about 45cm (18in) long.

How old are dolls?

Dolls have been around since there were children! At first they were very simple - just a piece of cloth with a crudely drawn face or a piece of carved wood or bone.

The Egyptians had dolls with movable limbs. In Roman times children played with rag dolls.

Greek clay dolls had cords attached to their arms and legs, so they moved up and down when pulled. The Romans had dolls' furniture made of lead, so they may have had dolls' houses too!

Up to the 19th century dolls were made of cloth and leather, often with hand-carved heads. In Europe, after the 1850s, dolls' faces were made with wax; heads and trunks of papier mache and cloth bodies stuffed with sawdust, which often trickled out!

The more expensive dolls had beautiful faces with heads and hands made of porcelain. They had long hair and glass eyes and were sometimes dressed in Paris fashions.

Who made dolls talk?

Two famous inventors gave dolls speaking voices. In 1827 Johann Maelzel, the German inventor of the metronome, put a voice box into a doll. When you gave it a squeeze, it said 'Mamma' and 'Papa'.

Later in the 1880s, Thomas Edison, the inventor of the phonograph or gramophone, designed a specially made phonographic cylinder small enough to fit inside a doll. A nursery rhyme was recorded on the tiny cylinder for the doll to recite.

Where is the world's longest wall?

The Great Wall of China is 2,400km (1,500 miles) long, 7m (23ft) high, and a roadway of 5.5m (18ft) runs along the top.

It was thought that this would be the only structure that would be visible from the Moon. We now know that nothing man-made can be seen at that distance.

Who built the Great Wall of China?

The first Chinese emperor is usually given credit for building the wall around 215BC. In fact, large parts of the wall were already 200 years old. Shi Huangdi ordered the sections to be joined together to keep out the wild Mongol tribes from the north. Hundreds of thousands of soldiers, slaves and criminals worked and died on the wall.

The Great Wall did not stop the Mongol army of Genghis Khan in the 13th century from invading China.

Who was buried with an army?

It was the same man, emperor Shi Huangdi. In 1974 workers digging a well near the tomb of the emperor found a life-size terracotta soldier. So began one of the world's greatest ever archaeological finds.

So far, 6,000 warriors, horses and chariots have been found. All are made in terracotta - originally they had been painted to look real, and were fully armed with real weapons.

What is terracotta?

It is clay baked to a brownish red, but not glazed. The name means 'baked earth'.

Who else built a great wall?

The Romans invaded Britain in AD43. Within 40 years the whole country was under Roman rule. The wild tribes of the north caused many problems, so the emperor Hadrian built a great wall in AD120-130. It passed through present day Newcastle and on past Carlisle to the west coast.

It had forts and watchtowers every mile along its 120km (75 mile) length. It was the most northern part of the Roman Empire. Parts of the wall can still be seen today.

What was the Roman army like?

The Roman Empire became the most powerful in the world because it had the best army in the world for hundreds of years.

Each man was well trained and equipped and fought in a well organised unit. Their enemies were mostly wild tribesmen who could not match the Roman fighting skill and discipline. The Romans were also skilled at building forts and bridges, so nothing could stop their advance.

A 'mile' castle, these were spread out along the length of the wall

What was a centurion?

The Roman army fought in units of 100 men (a century). Their commander was called a centurion.

Did you know the Romans used catapults?

They were large machines that could throw a stone as heavy as a man. Other types called ballista were big like crossbows.

Do you believe in Roman ghosts?

One of the strangest sightings of ghosts happened in the historic city of York in England.

A plumber was working alone in the cellar of an old building when he heard the blast of a trumpet. A Roman soldier on horseback came through the wall followed by a whole column of armed soldiers. The strangest thing was that the lower parts of the soldiers' legs were below floor level.

It was later found that the original Roman road was 50cm (20in) below the cellar floor!

Did Nero fiddle while Rome burned?

No! In AD64, a great midday fire destroyed two thirds of Rome while Nero was away at the seaside. He couldn't have played the fiddle either - it wasn't invented until the 16th century!

How many penguins live in the Arctic?

Penguins live in the South Pole - there are none in the Arctic at all!

Were the bagpipes invented in Scotland?

Romans played bagpipes in the first century and they were used in the Middle East, Persia and Arabia centuries ago. King Henry VIII had a set of his own, and folk tunes of Ireland, France, Spain, Italy, Russia, Scandinavia and, of course, Scotland, are often accompanied by the bagpipes.

What is Big Ben?

Big Ben is the bell that chimes the hours in the clock tower of the Houses of Parliament. It is not the clock itself! Installed in 1859, Big Ben rings out the hours after the Westminster chimes.

What is a coracle?

A wickerwork boat like a round canoe, covered in skins and made watertight with a covering of tar. Coracles were in use in pre-Roman times and they are still used in Wales today.

What does 'dead as a dodo' mean?

This phrase means totally dead - extinct! The dodo was discovered in Mauritius in 1507 and was extinct by 1681. This big bird with short wings could not fly to escape its enemies.

What is a Portuguese man-of-war?

It sounds like a galleon, but it is really a very dangerous type of jellyfish! Its poisonous stinging tentacles up to 25m (82ft) long can sometimes kill humans.

Was the yo-yo invented in America?

The toy came into the USA in the 1920s from the Philippines where the word 'yo-yo' means 'come come'. In the Orient and ancient Greece yo-yos had been popular for centuries.

How did the teddy bear get its name?

President Theodore Roosevelt was out hunting in Mississippi in 1902 when he refused to shoot a bear cub. The story was reported in the newspapers and after that the first toy bears were made, known as Teddy's bear.

What is a figurehead?

In the old days of wooden sailing ships, the builders would add a carved figurehead, often of a woman, on the bow as a ship's mascot. They were usually brightly painted.

Who was America's first president?

George Washington became America's first president on April 30 1779. He was a plantation owner, soldier and president for eight years. You can still visit his estate at Mount Vernon, Virginia.

Did he really chop down that cherry tree?

When George Washington's father asked his son if he had really chopped down his cherry tree, young George replied, "I cannot tell a lie!" Then he confessed. This story was made up years later by his biographer.

What was the Kon Tiki?

The Norwegian explorer Thor Heyerdahl built a raft of balsa logs - the Kon Tiki. In 1947, together with a crew of five, he crossed 6,900km (4,300 miles) of open ocean from Callao in Peru to a coral reef east of Tahiti.

It took 101 days, but he proved that Incas could have made the same journey 1,500 years ago.

What is a magnet?

It is a piece of metal that can attract or repel other metals. The ends of a magnet are opposite poles. One end will point to the North Pole, the other to the South Pole, this is how a compass needle works. If you put two magnets togther, North Pole to North Pole they push apart.

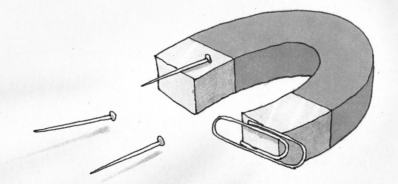

Why do hurricanes have names?

Because of an Australian weatherman called Clement Wet Wragge. When he quarrelled with someone, he named the next hurricane after them.

Now each year a list is drawn up of girls' and boys' names in alphabetical order, ready for future hurricanes.

What is a fjord?

Fjords are long, deep inlets from the sea, found in the glacial valleys of Norway.

During the ice age, glaciers cut these valleys, and when the ice finally melted, sea water flooded in.

What is a silhouette?

There was once a French statesman well known in the 1700s for doing things as economically as possible - his name was Etienne Silhouette. He gave his name to those simple black shadow portraits.

Who wrote Frankenstein?

Late one night on the shores of Lake Geneva, Lord Byron suggested his friends wrote ghost stories. So Mary Shelley, wife of poet Percy Bysshe Shelley, created the frightening monster Frankenstein - she was just 19.

Where does silk come from?

Silk is a fine thread produced by silk worms. A silk worm lays eggs on a mulberry leaf, which the caterpillar eats when it emerges. After a month they spin a silk cocoon around themselves. Before they can develop into a silk moth, the cocoons are taken and soaked in hot water to make silk and the pupa dies. One silk worm can spin up to 1.2km (3,900ft) of single thread.

What is the United Nations?

It is an association of nations set up in 1945, to help poor countries improve living conditions, to promote peace and international cooperation, and to uphold the rights of people of all races and religions.

The UN government headquarters (opened in 1952) is in New York, built on land given by John D. Rockefeller.

What is UNICEF?

It is the United Nations Children's Fund, founded in 1946 to help the children of the world. In 1965 the fund won the Nobel Prize for peace.

Who lives on a sampan?

Many Chinese live all their lives on floating, flat-bottomed wooden boats called sampans.

In some cities where space is limited, people live crowded together on sampans in big harbours. Some boats sell goods, others are used for fishing by day, and sleeping on by night.

Which insect can walk on water?

Many pond insects seem to walk on water. They do so because of the surface tension. The pond skater's legs press into a kind of elastic skin on the surface of the water - but don't go through!

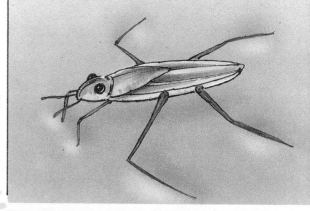

What is a sedan chair?

In the 18th century, wealthy people hired sedan chairs. They were carried through the dirty streets by two strong chairmen and this protected their fine clothes and elaborate hairstyles.

Where is the world's tallest structure?

The CN Tower in Toronto, Canada. This self supporting tower is 553m (1,814ft) high. It has a revolving restaurant at 347m (1,140ft). As you eat, you can see the hills 120km (75 miles) away.

Can you really hear the sea in a seashell?

You are hearing ordinary sounds echoing and re-echoing as the air inside the shell vibrates. Another roaring sound is the amplified sound of the blood rushing through your own ear!

Is the white rhino really white?
No - it is the same colour as the black rhino! It has a wide upper lip and grazes like a cow. The black rhino's lip is pointed for plucking twigs and leaves.

Why do opossums play dead?
The expression 'playing possum' means pretending to be dead. Opossums do this when trying to escape the attention of an enemy or facing danger.

Who was Queen Boadicea?
The Queen of an ancient British tribe, the Iceni. She led her followers in fierce and bloody battles against the Romans. In AD62 she was defeated and poisoned herself.

Who painted themselves with woad?
The ancient Britons dyed their bodies with woad, a blue dye made from the leaves of the woad plant. Their painted blue tattoos made them more fearsome in battle.

Where is the world's highest lake?
Lake Titicaca 3,810m (12,500ft) high up in the Andes. It is the longest lake in South America 190km (118 miles) long. The local Indians made reed boats from the reed forests by the lake.

What is the Statue of Liberty?

This is the huge and beautiful statue that stands on Liberty Island in New York harbour. She was made in France and given as a gift to America by the people of France.

How tall is she?

The figure stands at 46m (151ft) tall, but she stands on a pedestal of the same height, making her 92m (302ft) tall altogether.

Who built her?

The idea for the statue came from Edouard de Laboulaye, a French professor in 1865. He discussed it with his friend the sculptor Frederic Auguste Bartholdi, who later designed and built the huge figure which he called Liberty Enlightening the World.

It was 21 years later that the statue was completed in 1886.

Why is she green?

The figure is made of thin copper sheets beaten into shape over a frame. When copper is exposed to the weather it turns pale green.

Does her torch light up?

The original torch was lit from inside, but the light was very poor. Liberty was given her second torch earlier this century, but over the years it was damaged by rain.

In 1984 she was given a new torch covered in gold leaf. With spotlights on the outside it looks as if the torch is alight.

Where is there another statue just like her?

There is a smaller copy of the statue by the River Seine in Paris, which is where she was designed and built.

How tall is the Eiffel Tower?

This famous tower, which must be one of the wonders of the modern world, stands 300m (984ft) high and dominates the Paris skyline.

How heavy is it?

It weighs 7,100 tonnes, which is not very heavy for something so gigantic.

What was it used for?

It was built for the 1889 Paris exhibition as a rival to the Crystal Palace in London. It was only expected to last for 20 years, but it was so useful as a telegraph station, and later as a radio mast, that it still stands today.

What is the link between the tower and the Statue of Liberty?

The answer is the man who designed the tower, Gustav Eiffel. The statue in New York is made of thin copper sheets, but the huge size is supported by an iron frame inside. This was designed and built by the French engineer Eiffel some years before his famous tower. He became known as the magician of iron.

What famous cathedral is on an island in Paris?

The national church of France, Notre Dame, stands on the Ile de la Cité in the River Seine.

Did you know that the Louvre was once a royal palace?

Today the Louvre is the home of some of the world's greatest art treasures, holding 200,000 exhibits, but it was once the residence of the Kings of France.

Who built the Arc de Triomphe?

The building of this huge gateway was ordered by Napoleon in 1806. Beautifully decorated with sculptures, it took 30 years to complete.

Is there really a seahorse?

This small saltwater fish 4-30cm (1.5-12in) long looks like a tiny hobby horse.

It has a prehensile tail (it can grasp things) and it swims upright.

What is astrology?

There is a belief that events can be foretold by studying the position of the planets and stars in the sky when someone was born.

Astrologers refer to this part of the sky as the zodiac. The constellations of the zodiac are divided into 12 groups, each with its own sign.

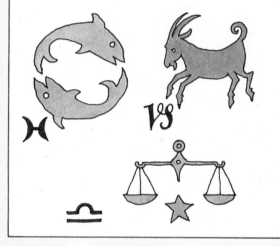

Where does the Red Cross symbol come from?

The symbol is a red cross on a white background, the reverse of the national flag of Switzerland.

In 1864 a young Swiss businessman, Henri Dunant, formed the International Red Cross, for the relief of suffering in war.

Nowadays, the Red Cross also provide relief in natural disasters such as earthquakes, floods and hurricanes.

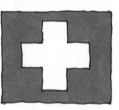

Swiss flag

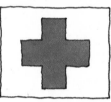

Red Cross flag

Which two countries play cricket for the ashes?

In test matches between England and Australia, the two teams play for the ashes, which is an urn containing the ashes of a burned stump.

The urn is kept at Lord's cricket ground, London - even when Australia wins a test series against England!

What is astronomy?

A science about the movement, distances and sizes of the Sun, Moon, stars, planets, meteors, constellations and comets within our and other solar systems.

Thousands of years ago some groups of stars were given names, because their shape was similar to a bear, a dog, a lion or perhaps a plough!

How useful is this tree?

Lots of products come from the coco palm tree. Boats are made from the trunk; leaves are used for thatching, basket making, mats and hats; coir fibre from the husks is used for ropes and matting. The coconut oil, milk and leaf buds are all edible products that come from this tree.

What are molluscs?

Molluscs are a major group of animals that include shellfish, snails and slugs. They have soft, limbless bodies with no skeleton - most of them are protected by a hard shell. Squids, octopuses and cuttlefish have internal skeletons.

Most molluscs live in the sea but some live in fresh water or on land. They are cold blooded.

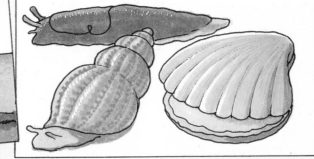

Is the croissant French?

In 1683 Vienna was under siege from the Turks. Men baking bread during the night heard the Turkish army tunnelling under the city. They raised the alarm, saved the city and baked croissants in the shape of the crescent Moon on the Turkish flag!

What was the Phoenix?

It was a fabulous bird of Egyptian myth. It lived for 500 years, built a nest of spices and burned itself to ashes. From the ashes came a young bird that lived for the next 500 years.

Where is the land of the Midnight Sun?

Lapland is a region mainly inside the Arctic circle. It stretches across the north of Norway, Sweden and Finland.

This is the land of the Midnight Sun, which shines continually for 24 hours a day, for 73 days from mid-May to the end of July.

Where did American Indians come from?

Until 20-30,000 years ago there were no human beings on the continent of America. The Indians are the descendants of Mongoloid people who crossed from Asia into Canada and slowly travelled all the way down to South America.

Why are they called Indians?

When Christopher Columbus arrived in America in 1492 he thought he had reached India! So he named the native inhabitants Indians and the name has remained.

What is a tepee?

The tepee is a large tent made of skins that the plains Indians lived in. Supported on long poles, they could easily be moved. The Indians of the south, such as the Apache, lived in a framework covered in branches, reeds or skins. They called this a wickiup.

Who were the medicine men?

They were the doctors of the tribe, but their main purpose was to deal with the spirits which the Indians believed were all around.

What was a peace pipe?

The peace pipe was a sacred object to the Indians. Called a 'calumet' it was usually made out of stone. All important dealings were sealed with the smoking of the peace pipe. To break your word after this would make the spirits very angry.

What was a tomahawk?

This was a light war axe. Until white people introduced iron, tomahawks were made of chipped stone tied to a handle.

Did the Indians always have horses?

Horses did not exist in America until the Spaniards brought them in the 16th century. It was over 100 years before the Indians had them. At first the Indians were terrified of the horse, but later they became the best horsemen in the world.

Do you know what moccasins are?

These were the shoes made by the women of the tribe. The tops were made of soft leather, often decorated with beads or dyes. The soles were of tough buffalo hide. They were stitched together with animal sinews.

How did Indian mothers carry their babies?

Babies were strapped to wooden cradle boards. They were highly decorated and were carried on the mother's back.

How did Indian families travel?

The Indians did not have the wheel. When they had to move, they made a sledge from two tepee poles drawn by a horse or even a dog. The sledge was called a 'travois'. As well as their possessions, elderly members of the family would travel this way.

Who first trained guide dogs for the blind?

During the First World War, a doctor at a German hospital left his German shepherd dog to look after a patient for a few minutes.

The way the dog behaved impressed the doctor so much that he began training dogs purely to help the blind.

Which tree can you hold in your hand?

Bonsai is the art of arranging and growing trees in miniature. The Japanese word 'bonsai' means 'they planted'!

With careful pruning over many years, these dwarf trees look exactly like a fully grown tree. Some are hundreds of years old and very valuable.

What is the spectrum?

Without light there is no colour. Sunlight seems to be white light, but it is made up of seven colours: red, orange, yellow, green, blue, indigo and violet. When sunlight passes through a prism it spreads out into a rainbow band of these colours, called the spectrum.

When sunlight shines through rain it is split up by the droplets into a rainbow.

Where is El Dorado?

A legendary city of gold supposed to exist in South America. A Spaniard thought he glimpsed a vast city roofed with gold, and since the 16th century many explorers have gone in search of 'the golden'!

Who was St Christopher?

In order to serve God, St Christopher carried travellers across a fast-flowing river.

One day as he was carrying a little child, he felt he had the sins of the whole world on his shoulders. It was the infant Christ as all the pictures of St Christopher now show!

What is karate?

The word means 'empty hands', fighting without weapons. Karate is a fast dangerous fighting sport using punches, kicks and throws. Originally from China, karate has been developed in Japan where the first school (dojo) was set up in 1924.

Karate can be used for self-defence or attack.

What is judo?

Judo was probably developed by Chinese Buddhist monks to defend themselves without hurting their attacker. By using holds, throws and falls the attacker's size can be used against them.

There are no punches or kicks used in judo, it is mainly used for self defence.

What was Pegasus?

In Greek mythology Pegasus was a fabulous winged horse, which sprang from the blood of Medusa, after Perseus had cut off her head.

Pegasus flew to heaven and a constellation is named after him.

How does a nettle sting?

The leaves and stem of a nettle are covered in microscopic sharp pointed hairs. A stinging fluid passes through these hairs and the flesh of anyone touching the nettle.

What do 'port' and 'starboard' mean?

In the days before boats had a central rudder they were steered by an oar called a 'steer board' on the right hand side.

To avoid crushing the steer board, the boat tied up in port on the left hand side, hence the names 'port' and 'starboard'.

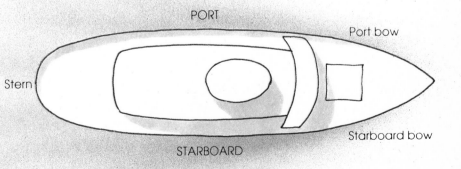

PORT

Port bow

Stern

Starboard bow

STARBOARD

What time is it?

Almost everything in our lives is controlled by time. Time to get up! Time to catch the bus! Time to go to school! We have clocks and watches that tell us the exact time to the second. But how did people tell the time in the past?

How do you tell the time with a stick?

Early humans noticed that as the Sun passed overhead during the day, shadows moved around. By placing a row of evenly spaced stones in front of a stick, the moving shadow measured the time passing.

What is a water clock?

The ancient Egyptians measured time by water dripping from a marked jar. The Greeks dripped water into a jar which made a float rise and turn the hand of a clock.

What is a sundial?

The sundial works just like the stick and the stones. People put them in their gardens or on buildings and tell the time by the moving shadow. The trouble was they didn't work in the dark!

Can you tell the time by candlelight?

Candles were once used to measure time. If you cut evenly spaced notches in the candle, as it burns down it gives a rough idea of the time.

Can you measure time with sand?

The hour glass was a good way of measuring time. It was in use for hundreds of years. Fine sand trickles through a small hole in the glass from the top half to the bottom. When the top is empty the glass is turned over. Tournaments were timed by the turn of a glass.

What is money?

Money, in the form of coins, notes or plastic cards, has a known value and can be exchanged for goods of an equal value.

The ancient Egyptians used gold and silver by weight. They would carry bits of silver wire or lumps of gold and cut pieces off. Other people had even stranger money.

Who had the largest money?

The people of Yap, an island in the Pacific Ocean, carved stone discs as money. Some were up to 4m (12ft) wide.

Who could eat their money?

In Africa salt is valuable, so bars of rock salt wrapped in reeds were used as money. Goods can also be bought with cattle or goats.

Who would pay with seashells?

Small cowrie shells were used as money in many parts of the world. They were known to be used in ancient China and in parts of Africa up to the last century.

Who made their money with beads?

The North American Indians made belts of beads called 'wampum'. These belts, like the stones of Yap were used to settle agreements between villages or tribes, they were not really for buying goods.

Who paid in axe heads or knives?

The ancient Chinese used tools for trade and their earliest coins were shaped like knives and hoes. These were difficult to carry and were replaced by round coins. Money axes were also used in Mexico. Made of copper, they were too soft to be real tools.

Who started the use of paper money?

In the 10th century the Chinese coins were made of iron and very heavy. People began leaving their money with merchants who would give them a written receipt for its value. The idea of paper money grew from this.

Where did the first Olympic Games take place?

These ancient games were part of a religious event, sacred to the god Zeus. They were held every four years on the plain of Olympia, at the foot of Mount Kronos in southern Greece.

Were the games held in special buildings?

On the site at Olympia was a great temple and altar to Zeus. Athletic events were held in the stadium, and races for horses and chariots took place in the Hippodrome. There was a wrestling ground by the river, a gymnasium and baths. Ruins of the site can still be seen today.

How many years did the ancient Olympics last?

The games lasted for almost 1,200 years from 776 BC until AD 393, when the Christian emperor of Rome, Theodosius I, abolished them. He said the games were pagan!

Which five events make up the ancient pentathlon?

Running, jumping, discus, javelin and wrestling.

What happened to Olympia?

Most of the buildings collapsed during an earthquake 1,000 years after they were built.

How did the ancient competitors dress?

They didn't! Ancient athletes wore no clothes at all when they competed in the events.

Did the Grecian women break any records?

None at all! Women were barred from competing in the games. Young girls were allowed in as spectators, but wives could be put to death for watching or taking part.

All competitors had to be male, of Greek descent and Greek speakers.

How did the marathon get its name?

Marathon was a town in ancient Greece. In 490BC a great battle was held there between the Greeks and the Persians. News of the Greek victory was taken 26 miles to Athens by a runner named Pheidippides, who fell dead from exhaustion as he entered the city.

The marathon commemorates his amazing run.

Which film star won five Olympic medals?

Johnny Weissmuller, who played Tarzan, won five gold medals for swimming in the 1924 and 1928 games.

How long is a modern marathon?

In the London games of 1908 officials added 385 yards to the 26 mile race. That meant the race would end exactly in front of the royal box, and King Edward VII would have a good view.

From then on the official marathon distance became 26 miles, 385 yards (42.195m).

When was the first women's marathon?

Women were not allowed to run an Olympic marathon until 1984.

When were the first winter Olympics?

They took place in 1924 on snow and ice in the French Alps at Chamonix, in the shadow of Mont Blanc.

Why does the Olympic flag have five rings?

Five interlaced rings on a white background represent the five inhabited continents: Africa, America, Asia, Australasia and Europe. The five different colours of the rings are decorative.

Are Olympic medals pure gold?

No! Olympic medals are made of gilded silver.

When did the modern Olympics begin?

They were revived in 1896. A Frenchman, Baron Pierre de Coubertin first had the idea, which he put before an International Congress of 15 nations in Paris. They agreed that the Olympic Games should begin once more and be held every four years.

Where did they hold the first modern games?

Appropriately, they were held in Athens. King George I of Greece opened the very first modern Olympic Games.

How many times have the games been cancelled?

During the two World Wars the games could not take place in 1916, 1940 and 1944.

Which five events make up the modern pentathlon?

Running, swimming, fencing, shooting and horse riding.

Who were pirates?

They were sea-robbers who attacked and stole from other ships and travellers on the high seas.

Piracy has gone on since people first sailed the sea. Ships of ancient Greece and Rome were often attacked crossing the Mediterranean. Vikings (the word means 'pirates') used to raid the coasts of Britain and Western Europe. During the seventeenth and eighteenth centuries pirates hunted and plundered ships across the seven seas.

Who was Blackbeard?

His real name was Edward Teach, but the name Blackbeard once struck terror into the hearts of anyone who sailed the seas.

His name came from his black waist-length beard tied up with ribbons. This fearsome man stuck slow-burning tapers under his hat, six pistols in his belt and a cutlass in his hand before swarming over the side of an enemy ship.

Who were the buccaneers?

They were sailors who had deserted their ships, escaped slaves, runaway servants, and men from different countries, and they all gathered on the island of Hispaniola (today known as Haiti and the Dominican Republic).

These men hunted the wild cattle of the area, which they killed for food. They hung thin strips of the meat to dry over special wire frames called 'boucaniers' or buccaneers. Around 1630 the buccaneers began to attack the Spanish treasure ships that passed their island shores. At first they used dug-out canoes. Later they built flat-bottomed sailing ships that could lie in wait in the shallow waters around the coasts of the Spanish Main.

How did Blackbeard die?

He was killed in 1718 after boarding Lieutenant Maynard's Royal Navy sloop. Blackbeard died after receiving five bullet wounds and 20 gashes from a cutlass.

Where was the Spanish Main?

The southern coasts of North America and the islands of the West Indies in the Caribbean were known as the Spanish Main.

Spanish galleons heavily laden with gold plundered from the New World often set sail for Spain, some were attacked by pirates and never reached home!

GULF OF MEXICO

SPANISH MAIN

What are 'pieces of eight'?

Spanish pieces of eight were silver coins worth eight reales. They were shipped in huge quantities between Europe and Mexico by the powerful Spanish empire. Commonly known as dollars, they and the gold doubloon coin were the main targets of pirates.

What flag did the pirates fly?

No one knows for certain whether pirates really did hoist the Jolly Roger. It is thought that most pirate ships flew a simple black flag and not the skull and crossbones!

Who wrote a novel about a pirate's buried treasure?

Robert Louis Stevenson wrote *Treasure Island*, which tells how a group of friends go in search of a pirate's treasure. They are betrayed by their own crew, who are really pirates headed by the notorious Long John Silver.

Who was the pirate captain in Peter Pan?

The blackest rogue of all - Captain Hook! He had a mean scowling face with dark eyes that glowed when he used his hook, for Peter Pan had chopped off his hand and thrown it to a passing crocodile.

Did pirates make you walk the plank?

Although pirate captains could be very cruel - often torturing and killing their victims - making you walk the plank seems to be a myth!

What are truffles?

Truffles are an expensive food delicacy used in the very best French patés. They look like large spongy walnuts and grow in the ground. Because they like to eat them, pigs are often used to find truffles.

What was tulipmania?

Although still one of the world's favourite flowers, when it was introduced into Europe 400 years ago the tulip caused 'tulipmania'. Rare bulbs were worth as much as a house, particularly in Holland.

What is the difference between rabbits and hares?

The hare is often mistaken for its cousin, the rabbit, yet it is very different. Hares are larger with longer legs, they do not live underground like the rabbit and are immune to the disease myxomatosis that kills many rabbits.

What are baby hares called?

They are called leverets and are born with a full coat of fur.

What is a Tasmanian devil?

This fierce animal used to live in Australia, but is now only found in Tasmania. About 1m (40in) long from nose to tail, it only comes out at night. It feeds on small animals, birds, lizards and even wallabies if it can catch them.

What makes bread rise?

Bread dough is made to rise by the reproduction of minute fungus cells of yeast. Add yeast to a sugar solution and it multiplies rapidly. When flour is kneaded with yeast, water and salt, the yeast generates bubbles of carbon dioxide and makes the dough rise, which retains its shape when baked in the hot oven.

Was Sir Isaac Newton really hit on the head by an apple?

The story of this great English scientist discovering the law of gravity by being hit on the head is not true, although it *was* an apple that started him thinking about gravity that led to great developments in science and the study of astronomy.

He also invented a reflecting telescope and it was Newton who first realised what causes a glass prism to split light into the colour of the rainbow, the spectrum.

The apple tree which started it all was blown down in 1820.

Who cooked an omelette while on a tightrope?

The great tightrope walker Blondin performed many daring feats, but one of his strangest was in 1862 at London's Crystal Palace. He carried a 23kg (50lb) stove out to the middle of the rope. After lighting it, he cooked an omelette, still balancing himself and the stove high above the crowd.

What is Stonehenge?

Standing on Salisbury Plain is the greatest relic of prehistoric times to be found in Britain. It is a circle of huge stones, which look like doorways. No one knows who built it or why. It was probably built around 1700BC and may have been a temple for Sun worship. Centuries later it was used by the Celtic druids for their ceremonies.

Who was the first Santa Claus?

Many people believe it was Saint Nicholas. He was the bishop of Myra in Asia Minor back in the fourth century.

One day this kind old man heard of a merchant who was too poor to give his three daughters money to be married. So St Nicholas dropped three bags of gold down the chimney of their house. Next morning the three girls found the bags of gold in their stockings, which they had hung up the night before.

That is why children in some countries hang up stockings hoping that Santa Claus will fill them with gifts.

St Nicholas became the patron saint of children, and his feast day is on December 6th.

What happens on St Nicholas's Day?

In some countries it is a children's holiday and St Nicholas brings his gifts on December 6th, three weeks before Christmas. Other countries look forward to the visit of Santa Claus on Christmas Eve, but some lucky children receive gifts on both days!

How does St Nicholas arrive in Holland?

On St Nicholas Eve, December 5th, a boat sails into Amsterdam carrying St Nicholas and his servant Black Peter. Good children get presents, but Black Peter chases the bad ones with his stick!

Santa Claus comes from Sankt Klaus, which was the Dutch name for St Nicholas.

Who leaves shoes by the fireside?

On Christmas Eve in France, children put their shoes by the fireside to be filled with presents by Père Noel or Father Christmas. In some parts of France they keep a yule log burning for all the 12 days of Christmas.

What happened to St Lucia?

Christmas in Sweden begins on December 13, which is St Lucia's day.

Long ago the early Christians were persecuted and had to meet in dark underground caves. St Lucia risked her life to bring them food. On her head she wore a crown of candles to light her way. One day she was caught by the Roman Emperor's soldiers and killed.

Today she is remembered each Christmas by young Swedish girls. They get up early on St Lucia's day, dress as she did to take buns and coffee to their families - who are still in bed!

What does the word Advent mean?

Christians all over the world celebrate Advent during the four weeks before Christmas. Advent means 'arrival' or 'coming', and people prepare for the coming of Christ on Christmas Eve.

What is an Advent calendar?

In Germany children look forward to opening the 24 numbered doors on this special calendar. Just one door is opened each day to find a small Christmas picture inside. The last one is opened on Christmas Eve.

Who hits a Pinata?

In Mexico all through the Christmas festival, children have great fun when they are blindfolded and hit a pinata with a stick. The hollow clay pinata jars are hung above the children's heads. They hit them with sticks, and when at last the jar splits, sweets and treats spill all over the floor!

Who are Julnissen?

In Scandinavian countries these are little elves who live under the floorboards and in barns. They look after the family and the animals.

On Christmas Eve, if a bowl of porridge is left out for these little fellows, they will come out and hide presents all round the house. If the porridge is forgotten, the Julnissen will play tricks on the family all the next year!

Who is Befana?

In Italy children wait for the good witch Befana. She rides over the rooftops astride her broomstick on Epiphany Eve or Twelfth Night.

She drops gifts for the good children down the chimney, and a piece of coal for the naughty ones!

What is the Epiphany?

This is a Christian festival celebrated on January 6th, when the Three Kings arrived in Bethlehem to bring their gifts to the Christ child.

What about the reindeer?

In America, England and many other countries, Father Christmas or Santa Claus has become the symbol of Christmas for children.

With his white beard and red cloak, carrying a sackful of presents over his shoulder, he travels from the North Pole on his sleigh pulled by reindeer. On Christmas Eve he rides over the rooftops and climbs down the chimneys with gifts for well-behaved boys and girls.

What is the largest state in in the USA?
Alaska! 1,478,425 sq. km (570,823 sq. miles). Twice the size of Texas, the next largest.

What was the first antibiotic?
Penicillin was discovered by accident by Alexander Fleming in 1928. Returning from a month's holiday, he found that mould growing on a culture plate had killed some of the harmful bacteria. The first antibiotic was named after the mould!

What was first on the Moon?
On September 14 1959, the Soviet Lunik II space craft crashed onto the Moon. It was the first man-made object to reach the Moon.

Where did golf begin?
It began in Scotland and was first mentioned in 1497 when King James II banned the sport. Men were spending too much time playing golf instead of weapon practice in case of war.

What is a cookie cutter?
A small shark, only 50cm (20in) long, which bites cookie-sized pieces out of dolphins, whales and rubber dinghies.

How many ants does an anteater eat?
The anteater tears the ants' nest apart with its powerful claws. Then he shoots out his long sticky, worm-like tongue and eats about 30,000 ants a day!

What is your pulse rate?
The average pulse rate of an adult male is 70-72 beats per minute. For a female the average is 78-82.

Which dog is named after a state?
The tiny Chihuahua dog was named after the state in Mexico. It is the smallest breed of dog, sometimes called 'ornament' or 'pillow' dog.

Which of the Seven Wonders Of The World still survives?
From ancient times only one can be seen and visited today - the Pyramids of Egypt.

Who took the first photograph?
In 1826 Niceephore Niepce took the very first photograph. It was of his barnyard in France. Dr Edwin Land's Polaroid camera took the first 'instant' snaps in 1944.

What is Esperanto?
An international language created by Ludovic Zamenhof in 1887. It is a phonetic language, easy for people of many countries to learn and understand.

How old is basketball?
In 1891 Professor James Naismith of the YMCA College in Springfield, Massachusetts thought of a game that could be played in a gymnasium. Basketball has been popular ever since.

When was margarine first eaten?
It was first made in France in 1870. The country was at war and butter was scarce. Napoleon III offered a reward for a substitute.

Who invented Lego?
Lego comes from the Danish words 'leg godt' which means to play well. Lego bricks were designed by the Dane Ole Kirk Christiansen in 1955.

Who made the first parachute jump?

Sitting inside a tiny basket, Frenchman André Garnerin, parachuted from a hot-air balloon as it floated above Paris in 1797.

Did spinach make Popeye strong?

In the 1890s nutrition experts put a decimal point in the wrong place and said that it contained ten times more iron then it did. It has no more iron for strength than any other greens!

Who was the human fly?

American George Willig climbed up the sheer face of tall buildings like a fly. In 1977 he climbed the outside of the 110 storey World Trade Centre, New York.

Who were the Pharaohs?

Ancient Egypt was ruled by a Pharaoh - a dynasty or family of kings. There were 31 dynasties, beginning in 4,400BC. The Pharaohs ruled Egypt for about 4,000 years.

Are canaries from the Canary Islands?

These brightly coloured singing birds are named after the islands, one of which was called by the Romans Canaria Insula or Isle of Dogs. Large dogs lived there and the Latin word for 'dog' is 'canis'.

Which film star broke a record?

When Johnny Weissmuller (Tarzan) was 18, he became the first man to swim 100 metres (328 ft) in less than a minute.

What is a pygmy?

Pygmies are races or groups of people who are less than 1.5m (59in) tall. The bushmen of the Kalahari desert and the Bambuti of the African Congo are pygmies.

Can fish climb trees?

The American mudskipper can as it goes in search of insects. They breathe air through their gills and use their front fins as feet.

Where can you find black swans?

They are native to Australia and live round the coasts and in the lakes. Only the tips of their wings are white.

Who invented the first vacuum cleaner?

When Londoner Henry Booth designed the first vacuum cleaner in 1921 he formed a company that would clean your house using his new invention.

What is a monkey puzzle?

The monkey puzzle tree or Chile pine with its branches covered in sharp scaly leaves is the only tree that a monkey cannot climb! It was brought from South America to Europe in 1796.

What makes waves?

Wind, earthquakes, explosions caused by underwater volcanoes, all make waves. Tides are caused by the pull of the Sun and the Moon.

Who was Jupiter?

Chief god of the Romans, his Greek name was Zeus. He had power over rain, tempest, thunder and lightning.

Who eats locust bread?

The Arabs dry locusts in the sun, pound them into a powder and bake them into bread. Sometimes they are fried in butter.

Which dancer named a cake?

The Russian ballerina, Anna Pavlova, had a delicious fruit-filled meringue cake named after her while on a tour of Australia.

Where is the largest amount of gold in the world?

There are 12,500 tonnes stored in the vaults of the Federal Reserve Bank of New York.

Who gave his name to America?

Although Amerigo Vespucci did not discover America, he described his voyages there so vividly that the new continent was named after him.

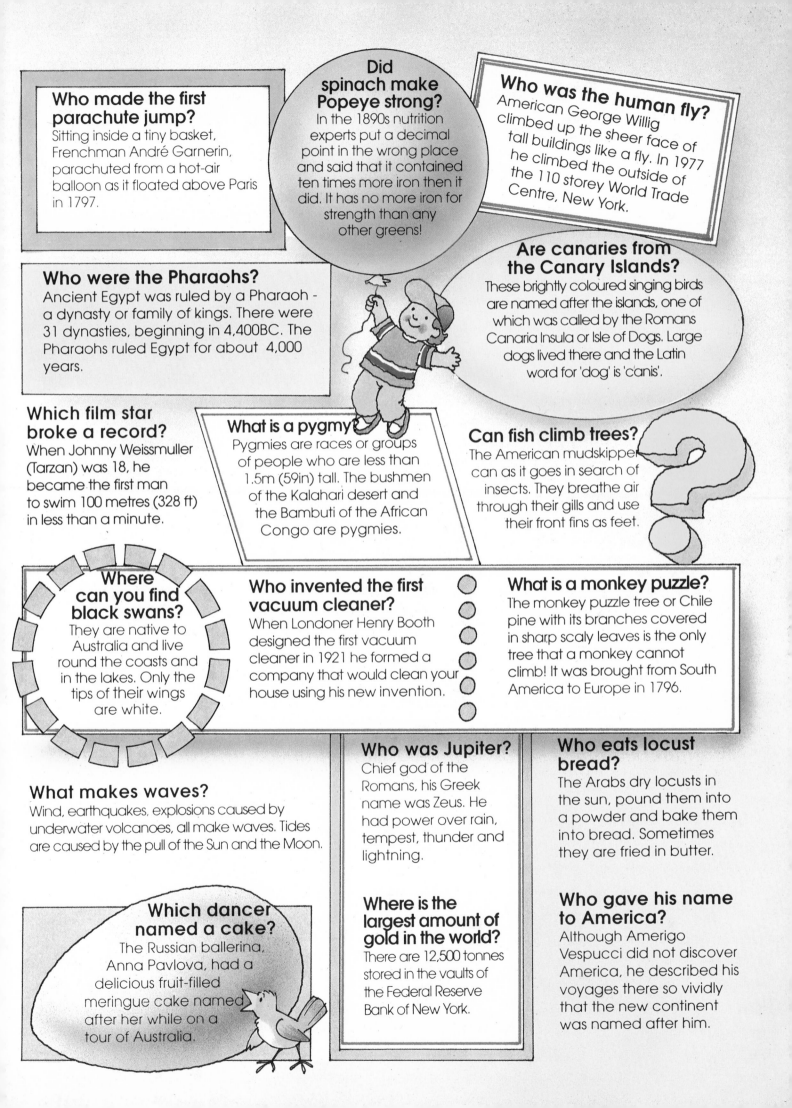